George Alfred Lawrence

Maurice Dering

Vol. II

George Alfred Lawrence

Maurice Dering
Vol. II

ISBN/EAN: 9783337039899

Printed in Europe, USA, Canada, Australia, Japan

Cover: Foto ©ninafisch / pixelio.de

More available books at **www.hansebooks.com**

MAURICE DERING;

OR,

THE QUADRILATERAL.

MAURICE DERING;

OR,

THE QUADRILATERAL.

A Novel.

BY

THE AUTHOR OF "GUY LIVINGSTONE."

IN TWO VOLUMES.
VOL. II.

LONDON:
TINSLEY BROTHERS, 18, CATHERINE ST., STRAND.
1864.

[*The Right of Translation is reserved.*]

LONDON:
BRADBURY AND EVANS, PRINTERS, WHITEFRIARS.

CONTENTS.

CHAPTER I.
UP IN THE HILLS 7   *PAGE*

CHAPTER II.
THE LAST LOVE 27

CHAPTER III.
CONFESSIONS 46

CHAPTER IV.
UNDER THE ELMS 64

CHAPTER V.
CONSPIRATORS 86

CHAPTER VI.
ON THE VERY VERGE 96

CHAPTER VII.
JUDGMENT 114

CHAPTER VIII.
EXECUTION 131

CHAPTER IX.

MISERRIMUS 147

CHAPTER X.

UNDER THE BEECHES 159

CHAPTER XI.

ANGINA 171

CHAPTER XII.

DE PROFUNDIS 182

CHAPTER XIII.

DARKEST OF ALL 194

CHAPTER XIV.

NO QUARTER 222

CHAPTER XV.

REQUIESCANT 237

MAURICE DERING;

OR,

THE QUADRILATERAL.

CHAPTER I.

UP IN THE HILLS.

LET us travel, now, a thousand leagues, Eastward Ho!

A deep irregular gorge; shut in on either side by a steep spur of the great mountain range that looms all around, dark against the sky-line; almost choked up, in parts, by low trees buried in creepers, and stubborn brushwood, and tangled grasses; with masses of a yellowish-brown stone cropping out here and there. Just such a scene, in fine, as you may see repeated, day by day, as you wander through the hill-country of India.

At certain points, when the rock comes too

near the surface, to allow rank vegetation to take hold, are small clearings, like a natural glade in our English woodland. Opposite to one of these, half-masked by a huge boulder, a hunter is sitting, with one rifle across his knees, another by his side.

We recognise an old acquaintance, though his cheeks look wonderfully tanned and brown under the white linen swathed round the close felt casque, and there is a burnt reddish tinge in his chestnut beard, as if it had passed through the furnace-heat of many fierce sun-rays. But the clear, honest eyes are not a whit changed, nor has one line of the face grown harder.

It is the same Maurice Dering, all over, whom you saw, two years ago, waiting on the 'rocketers' at Marston Lisle.

He is quite alone on his post; but two of his comrades are already ensconced in their several stations within a few hundred yards; for at this point it is almost certain that their game will break. It is a noted cover for bear; and they are to shoot at nothing else to-day.

Maurice's favourite *shikari* had been disabled early in that week by an accident. The man who ought now to have been at his elbow was a comparative novice in wood-craft. Old Kurreem would never have brought out bullets three sizes too large for the second rifle that now lay unloaded and useless by the hunter's side. Dering was noted for his success in managing his followers, whether actually in his service or not. The great secret of this was, that though always firm and decided in his manner, he never by any chance lost his temper with a native, nor condescended to use threats or abuse. On the present occasion he did not rebuke the lad's mistake very sharply; but simply told him to be more careful for the future, and despatched him to the tents, which were not far distant, to change the bullets; for neither of Maurice's comrades had any to fit that particular rifle.

The young *shikari* was silent and reserved, as are most of his kind; but his large bright eyes told plainly enough how he appreciated the Sahib's forbearance. He became famous in after-days; a bolder or more faithful henchman never trod on Indian soil. Was he thinking, I wonder, of that especial morning, as, years later, he lay, when all crushed and mangled they had dragged him from the tiger's fangs; when he took Maurice's hand in both his own, damp already with the sweat of the death-agony, and kissed it so thankfully and humbly; and then—glancing aside at the bloody writhen mass of brindled fur, that, awhile ago, was the dreadful Man Eater—went heavenwards with a smile on his thin lips, and a gleam of triumph in his black falcon eyes?

But if there was no displeasure or discontent on Dering's face as he sate there musing, it surely was much more pensive and grave than could be accounted for by the occasion. Indeed, it was evident that his thoughts were not, just then, with the game. He held in his hand an open letter, which had come to him that morning; as he turned the pages backwards and forwards, his brow darkened with anxiety.

That letter was from Philip Gascoigne; it was much briefer than usual; besides this, though it was as affectionate as possible, it was marked by a certain reserve and constraint that puzzled Maurice sorely.

"What on earth does he mean by that?" he muttered half aloud, as his eye lighted for the third time on one of the last sentences. "Surely he's not been ill; his wife would have mentioned it, even if Philip had kept it back. And what can have happened to worry him?"

The words ran thus:—

"This is the stupidest scrawl you have ever had from me. And I'm afraid the next won't be much better. I feel as if I should not be in real scribbling form for some time to come. Georgie must make her postscripts longer; that's all."

In truth, the postscript to-day was a good half of the letter: yet it did not convey any very important news; relating chiefly to the fair lady's triumphs at a certain fancy-ball, where she had appeared as Diane de Poitiers. She gave an elaborate sketch of her own costume, and mentioned, casually, that Captain Annesleigh's had also been much admired: he had been her partner in the *Moyen-age* Quadrille, in the character of the Second Henry.

Maurice bent his brows slightly as he read that last name; as men will do who are chasing some vague unpleasant recollection.

"Annesleigh?" he said, meditatively. "Of course; I remember. That's the man who backed me for such a cracker in the Grand Military. Pleasant enough to talk to; but not to be trusted, I dare swear. There are some ugly stories about him. I wonder if he visits much at Marston? If so, they are derogating fast. I've a good mind to give Philip a hint of what I've heard when I answer this. But Paul knows more about him than I do: he'll take care to keep everything straight. *That* Diana, too, of all Dianas——a nice character truly: I wonder they allowed her to take it." But his own frank smile came back to Maurice's lip, and his eye brightened with pleasure as it rested on the last paragraph of all.

"The Moor is *so* well. I see him every day, after breakfast, wet or dry. He likes me now better than he ever liked you. But he sends you his love nevertheless. And he wants you home again, as much as—we all do."

A very fair vision rose up before Dering as he read: a vision of golden tresses mingling with a black flowing mane; of a strong brown neck and swelling crest, bowed curvingly to meet the caress of a little white hand: just such a group as we fancy, under the torches, in the courtyard of Linteged, when the dawn of Duchess May's wedding-night was near the breaking; when the red-roan charger had so lately been lightened of his double burden; and the furious hoof-thunder had scarcely ceased to roll through the pauses of the rain,—

> On the steed she laid her cheek, kissed his mane and kissed his neck.
> "I had rather died with thee, than lived on, the wife of Leigh,"
> Were the first words she did speak.

Ever since he sailed from England, Dering had put his thoughts, on one particular subject, under very rigid discipline. They were, indeed, perfectly drilled now. Those postscripts no longer evoked that fluttering at the heart and quickening of the pulses that, at first, could not be denied or dissembled. If, in Maurice's recollections of Philip Gascoigne's wife, there still mingled a sentiment more tender than friendship pure and simple, they were surely guiltless of any taint of covetousness or repining.

Even so, O Benedict, my friend, may you sometimes think of the delicate white flower that you would fain have plucked in the days of your gipsyhood, had it not withered too soon, without treason to the Queen-Rose to whom you have since sworn fealty—that brilliant Beatrice, whose empire had been waxing stronger from the very day that she condescended to become your blessing and crown.

Yet perhaps it was scarcely prudent in Maurice to allow his fancies to stray as they did just then: the reins of the discipline whereof I have spoken were certainly relaxed for the moment; and the dreamer fell into a reverie, dangerously sweet in its very sadness. He could not refrain from one long, low sigh.

How that musing was broken, and how that sigh was answered, you are going to hear.

Whatever grounds he might have had for meditation on that especial morning, Dering was too thorough a sportsman to have yielded to a fit of abstraction, if there had been any immediate prospect of his rifle coming into play. The bears in these parts are generally very hard to move and loth to break cover; the beaters had not long got fairly to work, and their shouts still came faint and distant from the upper end of the gorge.

But Maurice's senses, naturally keen, had been so wonderfully sharpened by forest-practice, that a leopard would scarcely have stolen past him unnoticed, within fair ear-shot. A smothered, crackling rustle in the brushwood hard by was more than sufficient to recall those wandering thoughts, and bring him alertly to his guard. He was on his knee, quite ready for action—still half-masked by the boulder behind which he had been sitting—a full minute before the game broke cover in the clear ground before him.

He compressed his lips in silent disappointment, as two bear-cubs, about three parts grown, thrust their way through the tangled grass and branches, waving their brown-black heads restlessly from side to side as they blundered on, with the half-scared half-savage expression in their little bright eyes peculiar to their race when molested.

Maurice had hoped for a worthier antagonist. But he never dreamt of letting this chance pass. Besides, bears are very like men, and if allowed to run away, are pretty sure to fight another day, when it is not so convenient to other parties concerned. Hunting parties were not so frequent then as they are now, and the brutes were rather in the ascendant in these parts. So—muttering between his teeth " It's rather chicken-slaughter,"—Dering raised his rifle and fired twice in rapid succession. The leading cub rolled over, stone-dead and scarcely quivering; for the heavy conical ball had crashed right through its innocent young heart. The other dropped too, but lay tossing and struggling in a longer agony; the smoke of the first barrel hung slightly, and the bullet struck about an inch too far back.

Almost simultaneously with the last shot, Dering rose on his feet, and began re-loading with mechanical quickness and precision. But before lead touched powder, there was heard another sound, that struck rather startlingly even upon his nerves, inured as they were to all sorts of peril.

It was a savage, guttural growl, almost deep enough to be called a roar, half menacing, half piteous; in it spoke not only the fury of a wild beast hungry for battle, but the agony of a mother scenting the blood of her offspring. Neither was it the natural voice of the brute; for the Indian *ursa* is not prone to loud expression of emotion; and in the extreme of anger or pain rarely gives vent to more than a hoarse, grunting murmur. Then the tangled jungle broke away, as dry withy-bands yield to fire, and a huge she-bear crashed into the glade, rearing nearly erect, as she confronted her enemy.

Just such a figure, the children, shrinking and shrieking, saw issue from the wood of Beth-el, when their bantering of the bald-headed Prophet was about to be so incomprehensibly avenged.

It is very true that, compared to the terrible Grizzly of the Far West, the Eastern bruin is a tame, harmless animal: nevertheless, there are men alive who can tell you, that it is no child's-play when he closes in earnest: his claws are sharp and strong enough to tear a scalp away, as easily as you would strip a Tangerine orange of its rind. Remember, too, that the brute was maddened now by the philoprogenitive frenzy that makes the most pacific of living creatures bitterly dangerous.

But Dering's self-possession never deserted him for a second. He drove the ball home, strongly and steadily, and threw a cap on with inconceivable quickness: then he blew a long, shrill blast on a whistle that hung to his button; there was a peculiar note that gave at once to those who heard it the preconcerted signal of imminent danger. Maurice knew his comrades well, and could rely on help coming as soon as feet, swift and nimble, could bring it: besides this, he had one barrel loaded, and had great confidence in his shooting: so he awaited the onset in perfect calmness if not in comfort.

But, for a little space, the onset was delayed. After that first glare into his eyes the creature never seemed to notice her enemy: her whole attention was riveted on the cub that still lay writhing in the death-agony. It was pitiful to see her stooping over it, and fondling it with her head and fore-paws, moaning, all the while, as if her heart was breaking.

Unnatural and romantic as it may seem—to save his life thrice over, Dering could not have shot her just then. But he had not long to hesitate. All at once the cub ceased struggling, and, stretching itself out with a slight shiver, lay stone-dead. Before the last breath was fairly drawn, the old bear reared herself up once more, and, with a growl more terribly significant than that which had heralded her appearance, dashed in, straight and swift, to her vengeance.

During those few seconds Maurice had stepped back a pace or two, and stood now fully prepared. When the brute made her rush he brought the rifle steadily to his shoulder, and fired at once, sighting her right between the eyes. The bullet did not swerve from its mark one hair's-breadth, but the abrupt movements of the animal made the slope of the forehead uncertain; the ball glanced upward, inflicting only a deep flesh-wound that did not even stun.

Dering had just time to draw a short hunting-knife, and to throw his left arm up instinctively to guard his face and eyes: then man and beast went down together, locked in a death-grapple—the first-named undermost.

Some persons resuscitated from drowning have said, that a perfect diorama of past events and familiar faces passed before their minds' eye, during the last struggle for life. It was not so with Maurice: his recollections of what ensued were always remarkably vague. Yet, one thing he did remember. Over the growls of the savage brute above him—over the shouts of the men that were leaping down madly to his rescue—he heard, quite plainly, as if some mocking devil were whispering them, those last words that he read before he fell a-dreaming.

"And he wants you home again, as much as —we all do."

It seemed as though the weakness of allowing

thoughts to stray on long-forbidden pastures, was being punished right sharply, and with brief delay.

But all coherent feeling was soon merged in a strange excitement, which Maurice never chose to speak of in after days, and never could recall without shame. The simple truth was, that he was become drunk with the scent of blood in his nostrils—blood not all his own. The pain from the savage fangs and claws that ceased not to gnaw and rend his flesh—the horror of the hot noisome breath that mingled with his own— the happy Past, the dreadful Present, and the dim Future—each and all were forgotten in a brief delirium, not exempt from a fierce wild joy, as his right hand kept plunging into the side of his enemy, searching for the life that lay so deep. He did not even feel faint or wearied, up to the moment when sudden darkness swept across his eyes, while the weight above him seemed to grow more deadly heavy: after that, it was all blank and void.

The man who held the post next to Maurice Dering's was a major in the same regiment: he was not only a thorough sportsman, but a tried and famous soldier. One exploit of his in the Sikh war will not easily be forgotten.

He had been ordered to charge with his corps of Native Cavalry. Whether it was treachery or a sudden panic that affected the Sowars (who would fight well enough as a rule) was never clearly ascertained; but they began to rein up and fall back one by one, till, within two hundred yards of the enemy's front, the three European officers found themselves virtually alone. It was a critical time; for there had been some awkward mistakes made, of late, in cavalry movements. Those three men knew that death was before them, and dishonour behind: they never hesitated for a second, but rode straight on, with a cheer; breaking through the irregular line before them as they would have 'swished' through a bulfinch in the Shires. Reginald Errington came back with five wounds in him; and came back—alone.

But he said afterwards—he had no more vainglory in him than a child—that, while he was galloping on into the jaws of a bloody grave, he felt nothing like the faint heart-sickness that oppressed him, as he struggled over the few rods of rocky jungle that separated him from the scene of the death-struggle. When he reached it, he saw at the first glance that he had come too late to give any material aid. That confused heap, in which man and brute were mingled after a horribly grotesque fashion, weltered in a crimson pool—quite still and mute.

The heart of the strong swordsman, who had slain a human hecatomb on fairly stricken fields, melted within him, as he stood there, breathless and panting—more from excitement than exhaustion. He could find no voice to speak; and only signed to his own *shikari*, who had reached the spot nearly as soon, to help him to drag the corpse of the bear away. For a corpse it was; nearly drained of blood that had poured through three-and-twenty wounds. But for the other?——

In that inert, flaccid mass, livid white, save where it is furrowed with fearful gashes, who would recognise the strong hunter that went forth with the dawn, conquering and to conquer?

Reginald Errington turned away his face, and groaned aloud. Maurice had been wonderfully popular in his new regiment ever since he joined; but similarity of tastes in other things besides shooting had made him the peculiar ally of the man who knelt beside him there, with a dimness in his honest eyes, and a choking in his great bearded throat. The two had had some extraordinary days already, at the big game; and only the night before had been planning an expedition far into Cashmeer. And this was to be the end of it!

No,—not quite the end; for as the other hunter and some more of the attendants came up, Maurice stirred slightly.

Of all thanksgivings that have gone up to the Throne of Mercy, there never was one more sincere than the two syllables that broke from under the Major's huge grizzled moustache, as he sprang to his feet and called for "water!" Fortunately this was ready at hand: they dashed it over Maurice's face repeatedly; at last he opened his eyes, but closed them again instantly, and relapsed into a dead faint. Then they began to chafe his forehead and hands with brandy: so, after a while he revived slowly, and this time in earnest.

But the process of recovery was long; while it was proceeding, Ahmoud returned from the tents with the proper bullets. The lad's silent, stoical nature was quite transformed, for the moment, in the bitterness of his remorse: he would have it, that he alone was the cause of the disaster. Indeed, the first intelligible sounds that forced themselves into Dering's dizzy ears, were the wailings of the delinquent, as he imprecated curses on the graves of his deceased parents for having begotten so ill-omened a son; and the first decided expression on Maurice's face was compassion, as he turned his head, with a painful effort, to smile on the self-accuser.

He spoke, too, before any of the others, beginning in a faint whisper, though his voice strengthened rapidly.

"A sharp tussle; but I believe I'm all right, barring some deep scratches. *The bear's all right, too—isn't she?*"

Reginald Errington quotes those first conscious words of Dering's to this day, as an illustration of the strength of his own ruling passion; and I believe he would sooner part with the last of his ancestral acres, than with the rusty ragged-looking skin which he treasures as the trophy of that day.

CHAPTER II.

THE LAST LOVE.

The hurts, of which Maurice Dering spoke so lightly, though not church-door wide nor draw-well deep, were serious enough to confine him to his couch for many days. Yet he was recovering fast, when he, unluckily, caught the low fever prevalent in those parts, which threw him back again to death's door. When his iron constitution and case-hardened frame carried him through this last peril, he was fearfully weakened and altered.

It would have been difficult to find better quarters for a sick man than the bungalow to which Maurice had been carried as soon as he could be moved. It belonged to the chief magistrate of the district, who had arranged for Dering and Errington the *battue* that so nearly terminated disastrously: he was, indeed, the third hunter above alluded to, who has, so far, been left nameless.

Mr. Drummond was a civilian of the *ancien régime*, and represented that nearly extinct class very creditably. He came out as a griffin in those days when there was a real aristocracy in our Indian Empire—when its highest honours were almost hereditary in certain powerful families—when a Directorship was worth more than a close borough—when the Biennial Stakes for Competition-wallahs had not yet been founded. In spite of certain prejudices, and a punctilious regard for forms and ceremonies, peculiar to the school in which he had been brought up, few men in his Province were more respected and loved. Temperate as an anchorite in his own person, he was famed far and near for a royal hospitality; he discharged duties, varied and important, with untiring patience and rigorous impartiality, yet he always found time to carry out his favourite pursuit on a scale that few could rival; that unerring rifle of his had saved more than one life, and many a light-weight had reined up a beaten horse, while old Patrick Drummond, a hundred yards ahead, was drawing out the 'first spear.'

May the turf lie light upon his grave! For he was one of the very few, who, being themselves strictly virtuous, are solicitous that the rest of the world should not be stinted in their cakes and ale.

In this pleasant sojourn Maurice passed the long hours of a gradual convalescence. He rose up at last, almost himself again—physically. But some old feelings had utterly died within him, and new ones had sprung up beside. As he lay half-dreaming in the soft, cool twilight of his shaded room, his senses floating in the calm languor that ever follows a spent fever-storm, a wonderful peace seemed to possess him: he had not forgotten the past, or any of its ties; but all its pains and sorrows were as though they had never been.

In one word—the spring of the emotion that would, till very lately, stir within him at the sight of Georgie Gascoigne's hand-writing or the mention of her name, was broken for ever and ever. Passion he had vanquished long ago;

but never till now could he offer her friendship, pure, simple, and fraternal.

This negative state soon began to pass into the positive. If the sweet little sorceress had stood before Maurice again, wishing to re-knit the broken spells, she would have found herself powerless as repentant Maimouna. More than this—she would ere long have been aware of the presence of another fair White Witch, exercising gramerye more potent than her own; though it was innocent and holy—such as never was learnt at the feet of Magian.

Let us drop metaphor, and say at once that Maurice Dering—having had some trouble with his heart when left to its own devices—began to think seriously of handing it over, for safe keeping, to one that was right worthy of the trust.

Everyone wondered why Patrick Drummond had never married; but no one was disposed to quarrel with his choice of celibacy. No legalised mistress could have presided over the hospitalities of that pleasant house, more genially and gracefully, than did the widowed sister of its master. She had held the keys of office for many years;

and Alice Leslie, her fair daughter, had just come back to her from England, after a three years' leave of absence on urgent 'finishing' affairs.

I suppose, after severe illness this weak clay of ours is especially plastic and ductile, so that it will receive almost any impression, and retain it, sometimes, as it hardens once more. On no other hypothesis can we rationally account for the contracts entered into by certain of our brethren, weak though they may be. It is the same story over and over again. If you chance to marvel at one of these Mezentian matches, some friend of the family is sure to say—half apologetically—

"Oh, you know, her people were very kind to him when he was laid up at —— (naming some place 'on the further side of God-speed') with that terrible fall over timber."

Kind? From such disinterested Samaritans may Heaven keep me and mine!

Or—"He never would have got over that *malaria*, caught at Ancona, if it had not been for dear Lady Matchbury, who found him at the Albergo d'Espagna, quite by accident, as she was changing horses, and nursed him like her own son."

Her own son? Her son-in-law you mean. And—quite by accident, was it? As if we had not heard how the rotund mother and rubicund daughter stuck to poor Charlie Glenlyon's trail, through Germany, and Switzerland, and Sardinia, till they ran him fairly to ground in the Holy City at last! Did he not flee for his life, or—what he valued more—his bachelorhood, to Ancona, with a wild idea of taking ship from that unfrequented port to an unknown land; knowing that his only chance of baffling that staunch pair of braches was to 'take to soil?' By accident!—as she was changing horses at the Albergo? *Altro!* If that knowing and avaricious old aristocrat ever gave a double *buona-mano* in her life, it was to the postilion who drove the last stage that lay between her and her victim. Do you suppose that if Charlie had been clothed and in his right mind he would have yoked his fortunes to those of that stout and stridulous young person, who rolls when she walks, and screams when she talks, and squalls when she sings—he, who always raved about willowy waists and upheld a low, sweet voice as the most excellent thing in woman? Orazio mio! There are more philtres on earth than are dreamt of in your philosophy.

I confess that recollections of other's wrongs have led me far astray from my subject. These observations are singularly irrelevant: for no sort of unfair influence was exercised now on Maurice Dering. Indeed, any man, however wise, or stedfast, or strong of heart, might have been proud of winning sweet Alice Leslie.

The enchantment came over Maurice, not suddenly, but very slowly and surely. He began by feeling intensely grateful for all the small kind offices of womanly thoughtfulness that came specially from *her:* then he became sensible of a subtle attraction in her voice when she talked or sang. When the girl was playing chess with her uncle, her great brown eyes used often to turn from the game towards the invalid's sofa, to see if he wanted anything. After awhile each of these glances sent a strange thrill of happiness through Dering's veins; and he used to watch eagerly till another was vouchsafed him, and consider himself ill-used if it were long in coming. One day, a comrade, who had turned out of his way to see how Maurice fared, grew honestly enthusiastic on the subject of Alice's grace and beauty. After his visitor was gone, the invalid had a fit of bad spirits—not to say, bad humour—that lasted for some hours. It was not that he felt chafed, because that particular man chose to express admiration so freely. But he began to realize what a dreary thing it would be, if some one were to come and win the fair girl before his eyes, and bear her far away, so that they might never meet again till both were old.

On one especial evening he had begged Alice to sing to him; her voice was wonderfully adapted to the ballads in which Maurice especially delighted. At last, she opened "The Silent Land." The sweet, plaintive tones went straight to Dering's heart, seeming to beseech him not to palter longer with its secret. They were alone in the room, when Alice closed the piano, and came to his sofa to arrange the pillows;—Maurice took the little hand, as it wandered very near his cheek, and laid his lips thereon with passionate earnestness.

The virginity of a strong honest heart passed into that caress; for such an one Maurice had never bestowed on any woman, alive or dead. If his love for Georgie Verschoyle was mad and hopeless, it had at least the merit of keeping him pure and true.

That *this* love was not hopeless—if he had not guessed it before—he knew, before he unlocked his clasp of those slender trembling fingers.

Alice had heard her uncle so warm in Dering's praise, that she had been prepared to admire him before they met. The sharpest pang that had ever lighted on her innocent life shot through her breast, as she saw his face so drawn, and thin, and pale, when they carried him into the house from his litter. While she watched his recovery, her simple hero-worship had waxed into a deep, uncalculating, *womanly* devotion. If he had left her, without one word warmer than kindness and gratitude, she would never have reproached him, even in thought;

but it would have gone near to break her heart. No wonder that she felt faint with joy, when she knew that, 'henceforth, she might love without shame, and hope without fear.'

Though the happiness of this pair was never perfect till now, we will not tarry with them here, but march straight onward to our goal. Such 'passages' it is impossible to transcribe faithfully, unless they be of the staid and sober sort, which can interest only the parties concerned. Furthermore, I think that you will be glad that we did not linger over this scene, before all the story is told.

When Dering confessed to himself that it would be mad presumption if he nourished an idea of winning Georgie Verschoyle, he only looked his own position—and hers—fairly in the face. But circumstances were changed now. A troop in India is a very different thing from a troop in England, and will 'carry a wife' well enough; especially if—as in Maurice's case—there are moderate private means in the background. Neither could sweet Alice Leslie's matrimonial prospects be compared to those of a beauty-regnant at home.

Nevertheless, Dering did anticipate certain prudent scruples on the part of the elder powers. And so it turned out: he met, not with denial, but with demurrer.

Patrick Drummond was open-hearted and open-handed to a fault; but he had been born and bred north of the Border, and, at a pinch, could show himself both wary and worldly-wise. He was really attached to Maurice, and thought him fitter than any man of his acquaintance to be trusted with Alice's happiness. But he knew that his niece's own fortune would hardly have provided some women with their *trousseau*: he himself could help but little, for, having no occasion to lay money by, he had always lived up to the verge of his ample income. Besides, Alice was so very young.

Dering owned a godfather in England—an eccentric old bachelor with great possessions—who had already been very kind to him, in a capricious way: for instance, he made him a present of his troop. This reverend senior had a weakness for being consulted, whenever his *protégé* meditated any important step; it was more than probable that he would take serious umbrage if Maurice were to contract himself irrevocably, without previously advising him of such intention. The sagacious Scotchman could in nowise countenance the imperilling of such fair expectations.

For many months to come, regimental duty for Maurice was out of the question. Indeed, all the surgeons were inflexible on the point of his spending the next hot season at least in a more bracing climate than could be found anywhere nearer than the Upper Himalayas. In any case, it must come to a separation of the lovers for a period of several months.

In fine, Mr. Drummond decided (Mrs. Leslie, of course, played up to her brother's suit, as she had done all her life long) that Dering should go home, on eighteen months' sick leave, to be shortened to a year if circumstances should allow. Meanwhile, no engagement was to be announced to the world in general, though the parties principally interested might make what unauthorised contracts they pleased.

All this was so perfectly reasonable, and so very kindly expressed, that Maurice had not a word to urge in objection. A modified consent was all he had a right to expect; and this he had obtained, at once: so all the terms of the treaty were settled without useless discussion. If Alice Leslie's heart sank within her at the prospect of long loneliness, be sure she never murmured, even to herself; repining, now, would have weighed on her innocent conscience like wicked ingratitude. So she bore up bravely enough till the very day of her lover's departure; when she broke down utterly, and almost unaccountably.

When Maurice first saw her face that morning, he was painfully struck by its expression: not only sadness was there, but a vague terror as well; and the beautiful brown eyes looked wild and scared. That peculiar expression passed away very soon; but all the day long the girl was deathly pale, and she would start and shive at times without any apparent cause.

The lovers were never alone together till just before Maurice's departure, when the ruling powers granted one half-hour's space of undisturbed solitude. It is only with a few minutes of that solemn interview that we have anything to do.

They were standing on the brink of a deep clear pool, fringed with broad-leaved water-plants, and flecked here and there by ripples from rising fish; behind them rose a thicket of flowering shrubs, linked together by many chains of creepers, overshadowed by tall feathering palms; all round them was the whisper of the cool evening breeze, just then beginning to wake.

It was after a pause of some seconds that Alice spoke : there was a change in her voice; the tones that had been low and sad throughout were tremulous and awe-stricken now.

"I want to tell you something, dear, before you go," she whispered. "I know I am very weak and foolish, but you won't laugh at me—now or hereafter. Last night I had such a dream—ah, such a dreadful dream!"

The strong arm, that was wound so fondly round the girl's slender waist, could not avert nor arrest the shivering-fit that overcame her again.

Maurice bowed his head, till his cheek was laid on the smooth brown hair, and drew his betrothed closer to his heart; as if he would teach her where to look for rest.

"Tell me all, my darling," he said, cheerily; "even if it pains you—tell me all. You are not strong enough to carry a secret, though it be no heavier than an evil dream."

Alice stopped shivering then; she looked up in her lover's face, and drank a long draught of courage from those clear honest eyes.

"Yes, I can tell you, now," she went on in a firmer voice. "I dreamt we were standing together, just about this hour of the evening; only it was in England, I think, and we had no thought of parting. I cannot remember what words passed, but I know you were as kind and good as——you always are; and I loved you just as dearly. I think I was telling you so, when I saw a hand laid on your right hand—I was holding your left fast—that tried to draw you away. I knew it was a woman's hand—the fingers were so white and slender—before the figure showed itself from behind your shoulder. It was only a figure, for I never saw the face; something misty and black, like a hood, kept waving round the features, and kept them always in shadow. Yet, somehow, I knew that the woman was beautiful and dark and pale. And still she tried to draw you away, and still I held you fast, and I cried out—'Ah, Maurice, don't listen; tell her to leave you; tell her you are all mine.' And your lips moved, but no words came: and I felt that you were true to me, darling,—true all throughout,—but that you were under a wicked spell. Then I grew very strong and brave.

"'He *is* mine,' I said: 'by God's help I will keep him, in life or in death!'

"The figure dropped your right hand, and passed swiftly behind you, till she stood close behind me. Just then I became aware that we were standing on the brink of a chasm, so very deep that the bottom was a mass of grey vapour, and out of it there came smothered growls, as if wild beasts were chained there. Then the woman said in my ear (her voice was very sweet and musical, though she was so wicked and cruel):

"'If not mine, never—never yours!'

"And she pushed me over the brink before you could save me.

"And as I fell—ah, Maurice, hold me fast!—the growls from below rose into an awful roar, and the vapours swept away; and I saw a crowd of horrible creatures, something like men, with black faces and white grinning teeth, waiting to seize me. Can you wonder that I woke shrieking, or that I have been frightened ever since?"

Poor Alice's courage only just carried her through. As she spoke the last words she buried her head on her lover's breast, trembling like a netted bird, and broke into passionate weeping.

Maurice Dering was not in the least superstitious; and, as you know, his nerve was exceptional; but a painful thrill shot through him as he listened.

He had not forgotten a certain hour, just before sundown, when a woman—beautiful, dark, and pale—held his hand and sought to draw him aside from the path of honour, by proffer of her love. It is true, that he had no cause to look back at that interview with shame or remorse: nevertheless, the reminder of it, at that especial moment, savoured strongly of ill omen. There were unpleasant coincidences in Alice's dream. It was only by a strong effort that he could summon up cheerfulness sufficient for the emergency. He did not try to laugh the girl out of her terrors, but soothed and reassured her gradually by the gentlest endearments and caresses—as for promises, she needed none. At length, he succeeded perfectly.

When Maurice took his last look of that lovely face, lighted up by the last level rays of a westering sun, there were no tears there, save those of a natural sorrow: the sweet sad smile of loving adieu still lingered on her lips.

When he sees that face again, it will be radiant with another light; the tender lips will still wear a smile, but a smile of welcome; and there will be no traces of tears, that long ago have been wiped away, for ever and for ever.

CHAPTER III.

CONFESSIONS.

Let us see, now, how those who tarry at home are faring: to do this, we must look some months backward. The third October, from that in which this tale began, found Chetwynde and Luttrell once more at Marston Lisle. The two were crossing the park, on their way home from shooting, late one afternoon—Gascoigne had left them some hours ago, on pretext of business—when Geoffrey thus delivered himself of the results of long rumination :—

"There's something amiss with Philip, I'm quite certain. His shooting was never first-rate; but did you ever see anything like it, this morning? It wasn't only that he missed almost everything; but he shot so wildly. You must have noticed it, Paul?"

"I did notice it," the other said, gravely.

"And Philip was aware of it too. I never saw him vexed before, about his own misses. Don't you remember, that I never chaffed him once, all through the morning? That was the reason of my forbearing. Yes, there *is* something on his mind; and it's very unlike Philip—keeping his griefs to himself. I wish we could guess, without asking him a point-blank question. Do you think he can be getting uncomfortable about Annesleigh? I don't believe the little woman means any harm; but I wish he wasn't coming here next week. There's a taint of sin in the atmosphere wherever that smooth-spoken desperado happens to be. It will be a good day for honest, or comparatively honest, people, when the Devil claims his own. Gerald must have been waited for, *down there,* this many a year."

The parson shook his head remonstratively.

"Hush, Paul," he said; "harsh words won't help us, much less blasphemous ones. What do you or I know about the time when a man's soul is due? Annesleigh is as bad as bad can be, I daresay, if half the tales about him are true. But perhaps Marston itself is the real temptation to him. So few reputable houses are open to him now. At least, I never saw anything——"

"Of course you never saw anything," Paul broke in, rather crossly. "You never do. Why don't you ask Ida about it?"

Geoffrey turned short round on the speaker, with a comic perplexity in his broad blue eyes.

"There's no pleasing you people," he said. "My dear Paul, I *did* ask Ida about it—once. If it's all the same to you, I won't repeat the experiment. She never was so near being really angry with me. She has a knack, you know, of putting people into false positions, when they vex her. In about five minutes I felt a thorough scandal-monger, though I started with the best intentions."

Chetwynde shrugged his shoulders, as was his wont when he did not think it worth while prolonging a discussion, and walked on in silence. But, when they reached the house, he left Geoffrey to settle the morrow's programme with the head keeper, and went straight to

Gascoigne's *sanctum*. Philip was sitting in a low arm-chair, drawn up close to one of the windows—his head leant on his hand, and turned towards the darkening landscape—evidently rather drowsy, or in a deep reverie; for he never moved at the sound of the opening door, or the entering footstep.

Now, that same hour of equinoctial twilight—if you happen to be in weak health and poor spirits—is a very trying one to encounter, alone. The phantasms that arise, then, are seldom ghastly or terrible, but they are inexpressibly dismal and discouraging.

The peculiar light and the peculiar attitude may have had something to do with it, but the instant that Paul crossed the threshold he knew that his suspicions, relative to some unknown trouble of Gascoigne's, were only too well founded.

Philip never rose till his friend's hand touched his shoulder: then he raised himself with a start, and began to ask hurried questions, as to the sport since he left the others, &c. &c.

Chetwynde answered all these with perfect

composure; then he led up, quite naturally, to the arrangements for the following week.

"We can't beat that ground of Durden's till Thursday," Philip observed. "It's about the best we have, for mixed shooting; and Annesleigh only comes in time for dinner on Wednesday."

Paul drew up a broad footstool close to Gascoigne's elbow, and sat down before he replied—deliberately—

"Annesleigh comes on Wednesday?—to be sure he does. Now—Philip, old man—well as I know you, I don't want to interfere, impertinently, with your family arrangements. But just let me ask you one question. Do you think that's a nice sort of man to be running tame about a house? I happen to know, that he domesticates himself with extraordinary rapidity."

Gascoigne turned half round, and looked at the speaker with a languid wonder.

"Why, I thought he was one of your favourites, Paul," he said. "The only time I ever saw him, before I married, was in your chambers.

And he's always quoting you; as if you met perpetually in other places than here."

Chetwynde ground his teeth impatiently.

"He is not an especial favourite of mine, though I meet him often enough: and if he quotes me, it's as Somebody quotes Scripture—for his own ends. But that's not the question. What does it signify whom *I* herd with? I was speaking of 'houses,' not of 'chambers,' and of people who have ties and duties to attend to such as I shall never own. Once more, Philip—I don't want to be impertinent—but do you think you are wise in letting such a marked black sheep run at large about the Marston pastures? He's been here pretty often of late."

When he turned round once more, vexation mingled with surprise was on Gascoigne's face. It was not that he objected in the least to Paul's interference; but he was evidently sorry that his friend should disquiet himself in vain. He knew right well that Chetwynde never spoke thus earnestly, without bitter earnestness at heart.

"Don't be absurd, Paul," he said quietly. "You never *can* meddle 'impertinently' here.

Were you not sworn in of the privy council long ago? I believe the honour of Marston is just as dear to you as it is to me. But you do look at things, and people, too much *au noir* at times. I don't admire Annesleigh particularly, and never should trust him too far; though I think he has been trying to become more respectable for some time past. He told me, the other day, that he was 'going into steady training for the Upper House.' There may be some truth in it, for his uncle's health fails more and more. I've never heard of his getting into any scrape for the last two years; that's negative praise, anyhow. He's always an ornamental piece of furniture, you must admit; and he will be especially useful just now for these *tableaux* which are to eclipse the Molton ones. After all—who is in danger? Annesleigh has never tried to borrow money of me: he amuses Georgie; but I don't think she even flirts with him. If she did, I am sure I should have heard of it."

These last words were spoken in such perfect simplicity and good faith, that Paul would hardly have had the heart to hint a suspicion, had he entertained such, which really was not the case.

"Perhaps I *am* unjust," he said, slowly. "But you've heard the proverb about pitch as well as I have. It would be a pity if the scandal-mongers should see a speck on your wife's white hands, though you and I know them to be as stainless as snow."

Gascoigne threw back his head, rather disdainfully.

"The scandal-mongers! If *we* cannot afford to defy them, we have lived all our lives in vain. But, Paul, you are wrong again, here. It was not Georgie this time who suggested that Annesleigh should be invited, but Ida. I thought she was curiously eager about it, when she spoke to me."

Chetwynde whistled, long and low.

"Ida, was it?" he said at last. "That alters the case materially. If it comes to a match between her and Gerald, I should like to back her, at odds. I think she has that race, with several pounds in hand. There's not another woman in England that can take care of herself so thoroughly."

This was the deliberate opinion, remember, of a man endued with no ordinary perspicacity; founded, too, on the familiar experiences of many years. In good truth, the miscalculations of science are often more wonderful than the blunders of ignorance, and lead the judgment much farther astray.

So, for a few seconds, Paul sat silent and pondering. One thing was evident, Gerald Annesleigh was not the *bête noir* that haunted Gascoigne; yet that something weighed heavily on his mind was equally clear. Even during that brief interval Philip had sunk back into his old posture of listless melancholy; and though objects were barely distinguishable, his eyes had reverted to their dreamy outward gaze. At last Chetwynde leant forward, laying his hand lightly on the other's shoulder,—the room was nearly dark now,—and spoke, almost in a whisper.—

"Won't you tell me what it is? You know *anything* is safe with me."

Philip shivered slightly, but did not attempt to shake off the kindly pressure.

"It must come, sooner or later," he said, in his own low, musical voice. "As well now as at any time. My dear old Paul, you don't deceive me with your cynicism; what I've got to tell, will hit you as hard as any of them. Have you never guessed that, for months past, I've been getting weaker and weaker, and more and more blind? I could not tell rabbits from hares, to-day. I've tried to delude myself into thinking that it was only the old *malaria* bothering me again. But delusions are over, since I saw Ferrand last week in town. He cannot quite define the nature of the disease, but he told me fairly—he don't mince matters, you know, and I like him the better for it—that there is something radically wrong with the spine."

The hand that rested on Gascoigne's shoulder shook like a dry leaf in a strong breeze, and through the gathering darkness there broke a sound strangely like a sob; it came, not from the breast of the last speaker, for—his confidence once made—he sat mute and statuesquely still.

"My God!—is there no hope?"

The force that Chetwynde put upon his voice, to prevent it from failing utterly, made it unnaturally hard and cold.

"Of ultimate recovery—little or none," Philip answered, quite steadily. "But the decay may be very gradual, and I may linger long between the different stages; this, the first one, is generally more rapid than any, except the last. I never had much nerve, you know; but I think I should have borne up better, if it had not been for thinking, what a trouble and burden I shall most likely be to everyone that I wanted to make happy. That's very, very hard. God help me! I cannot see my way through the darkness."

"And your wife knows nothing of this?" Paul asked, still in the same hard, constrained voice.

"Not a word," Gascoigne answered eagerly; "and I trust to you to help me here. The secret shall be kept from her as long as I have strength to stand upright. My own sweet Georgie! Imagine her being condemned to humour a sick man's fancies, and watch the changes of his pulse. Six months of nursing would take all the bloom from her beauty. And is she not lovely now—and happy, too? The world never saw such a charming *châtelaine*. She shall enjoy the last month of our plenty, as royally as the rest, though the famine-years must needs come."

The twilight deepened more duskily, yet the pale, delicate face seemed to brighten. In truth, there was a light upon it, that has hovered, ere this, round the brow of others, whose spirit was as strong as their flesh was frail to endure— a light that shone, perchance, in dark, damp, amphitheatre cells, when, without, the sun glared down on crimson sand, and the voice-thunder out-roared the lions.

You may call this comparison over-strained, or irreverent, if it so please you. I write as I believe. I believe that, though the age of miracles is past, the age of martyrdom will last till the death of Time. I believe that some now living—though their suffering was not for conscience-sake—who have borne their heavy cross unrepiningly and unselfishly, will, one day, not stand far from the foremost rank of the Noble Army.

The change on Gascoigne's face did not escape Paul Chetwynde; he understood and appreciated it, thoroughly. The last barriers of his calm philosophy—they were but flimsy out-works after all—gave way, and his strong, earnest nature broke out. He dropped his head on his hand, and groaned aloud.

"And—with all this on your mind—you can be anxious about the *tableaux* they are to act next week, and can settle what ground we are to shoot to-morrow? Ah, Philip, Philip! you put the stoutest-hearted of us all to shame. And if the worst come to the worst—though I *will* hope for the best—do you talk about being a burden to any one? You never were really ungenerous, in all your life before. I'm not going to speak of Geoffrey; nor of poor old Maurice, if he ever comes back; nor of Aunt Nellie; nor even of your own wife, to whom you do scant justice, dearly as you love her. I'm going to speak of myself, if you've patience to hear it."

Gascoigne did not answer, it was too dark now for the other to see his eyes, but he drew Paul rather closer to him, by the hand that still rested on his own shoulder.

"Listen, then," Chetwynde went on, quite calmly now. "You know as much as any one of my past and present, but you don't know all. It would do you no good to know it, or I would tell you every word. It's enough to say, that it stands thus with me: I sit here, with four-and-thirty years told, and neither duty nor honour binds me to any living man or woman—not duty, because there is a wall built up for ever between the Dean of Torrcaster and me; not honour, because I never have asked, and never will ask, any woman, gentle or simple, to share such an existence as mine. Philip, I don't hope much, or fear much, for reasons that you may easily understand; but—I *believe* less, for reasons, or no-reasons, that you have been spared the knowledge of. I'm not going to make my moan now; or attempt to lighten your burden by weighing it against my own : one is physical, the other moral; the comparison wouldn't stand for an instant. But if you only could guess the dreariness of having nothing *absolute* to rest upon—no unalterable and incontrovertible creed. If you have not this, the subtlest disputant gives you your *Fiat Lux*. It is not enough to believe in a Supreme Being—I do that—you must worship Him after set forms and ceremonies: you must believe His written, no less than His unwritten words. I struggled hard—I swear I did—struggled like a drowning man, when those doubts and disgusts first came upon me; for I guessed what it would come to; but they beat me, at last. I've thrown up my hands, now, and float where the stream chooses to carry me. Did you ever hear me cavil at another's religion, or try to draw any one into controversy, or even scoff at fanaticism? I'll tell you why I never did so. I'd sooner see a man a confirmed drunkard, or gambler, or profligate, than a sceptic. There's a chance of recovery, if ever so faint, for all the others; for the last—none. Do you want to know whose fault it is, that I am what I am? My own, I suppose. At least I accuse no one, nor will I ever. There: I told you I should try your patience. You are my only confidant, and I don't think I should have spoken out—even to you—but for this. I want you to realise, how utterly alone I stand in the world. Isolation is independence, at all events. Once more, I would not interfere with those who have a better right to take care of you. But, understand, from this time forward, so long as you and I shall live, you have only to say 'Come' and I will be with you as quickly as steam can bring me, and stay by you till you tell me to go. Promise me this, at least: you will not scruple to use my hands and eyes, if your own should fail?"

Gascoigne sighed heavily; there was a deeper melancholy in his voice as he answered, than when he had been speaking of his own sorrows.

"Poor Paul! I never guessed at this. It is very dreadful. You are ten times more to be pitied than I. But though what you have told me has pained me more than I can say, it has not made me distrust you a whit. Here is the proof. There's the draught of a fresh will in the house now, where you are named as Cecil's first guardian, should he be left fatherless. I sign and seal that will to-morrow. And, otherwise—as you say, so it shall be. While we both live, I'll never scruple to ask you to help me at my need. As to what has passed to-night, do you keep my secret—as I will keep yours—till the time comes when it *must* be told. 'Unto the day the day:' perhaps for both of us there are better things in store than we dream of now."

So with no more words, and only one brief hand-clasp, those two plighted their faith. A hundred seconds later, when lights came in, not a ruffle of emotion on either face betrayed that between them there had passed almost the saddest confidences that man can entrust to man.

All that autumn through, the gaieties went on bravely at Marston Lisle.

The *tableaux*, before alluded to, were eminently successful, utterly eclipsing the glories of Molton; the most picturesque of them all was ' Sir

Galahad's Dream,' wherein Gerald Annesleigh (save the mark!) played the Maiden Knight; while Georgie, and Ida, and two other damsels almost as fair, watched his sinless slumber.

So autumn glided pleasantly into winter, and still Philip Gascoigne's secret was kept. Nearly a year must pass before you meet any of these our characters again; but when they next appear it will be *en masse*, and—for your comfort— they will be 'forming up' for the strong business of the last act.

CHAPTER IV.

UNDER THE ELMS.

A soft still evening follows a broiling August day. The air is fresh and cool; but, even now, there is no rustle in the leaves of the solemn elms. To meet or find a breeze, you must mount some hundred feet, and couch among the heather, on the crest of one of the hill-ramparts that fence in to the north the long rambling street of Spa.

The season is at its flood, just now; almost every civilised nation has sent hither traders or travellers, to buy or sell, or look at the raree-shows of the tiny Vanity Fair.

Here is Princess Czernikoff, the white sorceress of the Ukraine, who, for thirty years or more has kept alive her terrible renown. There were wicked whispers about her before she stood at the altar—a bride, in her eighteenth summer.

What was the story about her father's handsome secretary, who was such an accomplished musician? He was a serf to be sure; and serfs have no business to play false notes at state-concerts; yet it surely was hard measure, to make him shriek his life out under the knout that night of the wedding. Since then, for that pale, green-eyed woman, in half the countries of Europe men have drawn swords and died; and she will do more mischief yet, though she verges on the grand climacteric. Wherein lies the secret of her fatal fascination? The world in general, and her rivals in particular, are never tired of asking that question. Simple as it seems, it has never been answered yet. The Czernikoff's victims tell no tales.

Here, too, is Sofie Lichnöffsky, the lovely Polonaise, almost as celebrated and dangerous in her way; who has become *quite* irresistible since she grafted the patriot upon the coquette. When the languishing look in those glorious dark eyes is more *prononcé* than usual, her friends say it is the natural melancholy of an exile and martyr; when she falls into a fit of abstraction (as she will do when the converse interests her not) she is supposed to be meditating on the wrongs of her country. Of course, both on political and private grounds, she and the Czernikoff are mortal enemies. Neither will accept of divided male allegiance ; it is clearly understood that the briefest interchange of courtesies with the enemy, will be treated as desertion under arms, for which there is no forgiveness. The star of Poland is rather in the ascendant just now; for Sofie has succeeded in seducing from the opposite camp one of its chiefest paladins—an extraordinarily handsome Magyar, whose iron constitution and enormous revenue may possibly last about five years longer, at his present rate of expenditure.

Here, too, is the fair Fitz-Eustace, who has only lately abdicated the sovereignty of Southern beauty in favour of her fairer daughter. It is so ong since they crossed the Atlantic, that they must have forgotten the sound of the rollers. There is a husband and father 'out there'— quite orthodox and authenticated—who ministers lavishly to their numerous requirements; but the worthy planter dwells peacefully among his own black people—deferring, from year to year, the pleasure of seeing his Carolina Roses in bloom.

Nor is Hélène de Lauragais—*née* Du Château-Mesnil—absent; the eloquent *Marquise,* who can talk as fast with her eyes and her lithe fingers as with her pomegranate-flowers of lips. It is whispered that a certain Great Personage has looked upon her of late with favouring eyes; since that report—true or false—prevailed, the fair dame's social importance has become almost oppressive to her; for her frank, gay spirit is prone to recreate itself in the amusement of the hour, and is not often troubled with *arrière-pensées.* Now, whithersoever she may bend her steps in these her summer pilgrimages, certain grave and reverend seigniors, representing each some European cabinet, are sure to cross her path accidentally. It is not bad sport to watch her, responding to the stiff courtesies of some grey-headed statesman, whom even the reckless *Marquise* cannot afford to dismiss off-hand—her eyes flashing impatience all the while,

—her tiny foot keeping time to a favourite *valse*, now drawing very near its end.

So much for the womankind. The men are not worth wasting many words upon. The usual lot is fairly represented.

Mendez, the colossal Spanish gambler (who, if he plays square at any game—*Trente et quarante* included—is the most maligned innocent in Europe), has come across for a week's change of luck from Homburg, where two unlucky (?) croupiers running have made a large gap in half-a-million of winnings. He punts in just the same form as ever; placid and imperturbable while fortune favours; clamorous and quarrelsome when the tide fairly turns: a *roturier* from head to heel.

Look across the board of green cloth and you will see a refreshing contrast. That sallow man, with sharp, projecting features and weary eyes, who looks forty though he was a legal infant twenty months ago, is the great Belgian magnate, Prince Amadeus LXVI. You see he plays quite as high as the Spaniard, but does not deign to cast down his own *rouleaux*, or amass his own note-piles : all that is done by the grave secretary, behind whose chair the Prince stands, apparently a disinterested spectator, though he will murmur now and then, without bowing his head, certain mandates as to the game. That youth, at least, *se ruine en grand*.

Then there is, as a matter of course, the stout English *millionnaire*, who could buy up the whole Redoute—including the Bank—if it so pleased him; playing for five franc-pieces, or louis at the most; bursting into a sweat of agony if he loses thrice consecutively, and getting purple with triumph if he follows a *série de cinq* on his kindred colour.

You don't care to hear about the Italian with the fierce brigand-face and silky manner, who has always lost his last available *scudo* just before you met, when on the point of realizing a fortune by the marvellous martingale that only wants capital to be infallible? Nor of the venerable man, with the long white beard, and devotional aspect, who always crosses himself when he sits down to play, and then places by his card a small slip of dry wood, which might be a holy relic, if it were not a slip from the tree at Homburg, where, last summer, they found the Russian suicide hanging? Nor of the ancient female—rather the reverse of venerable—who will punt away for hours at a time, without once intermitting a dreadful mumbling murmur, that issues from under a cavernous black bonnet, like an oracle of Trophonius? You never guessed of what nation or language she could be, till last Sunday that portentous head-gear nodded close to your elbow, and you heard that malignant grumble still going on, as if a witch had strayed into the tabernacle unawares, and felt it incumbent upon her ceaselessly to curse the clergyman.

No—these personages might make rather curious studies in their way, but with them we have little or no concern. We are more interested at present in that group sitting under the elms at the lower end of the *allée* on this same August evening. Almost all the principal actors in this drama of ours are there; though Geoffrey Luttrell is absent, as he was through its opening scenes.

The most prominent figure—simply because it is so sadly changed—is that of poor Philip Gascoigne.

He had borne up, as he said he would, to the outermost verge of physical endurance; but, months ago, it became impossible to keep up appearances longer; the daily effort perhaps only hastened the break-down: he is a confirmed invalid now, and can only totter a few paces without the help of a strong arm. He had no pain to suffer, beyond the misery of utter lassitude and prostration; and he kept up his spirits wonderfully: indeed, he had seemed better in every way since he had been at Spa, after the fatigue of the journey was once got over.

Close to Gascoigne's shoulder sat Maurice Dering; a trifle thinner than of yore, with a white scar here and there showing through the deep bronze of his cheeks and lower brow: for the she-bear's claws scored sharply where they *did* come home. He had been terribly shocked on his return, to find Philip in such a condition, for he had not received the slightest intimation of it; but—thinking for his friend very much as he would have thought for himself—he decided that to brood over things was the worst possible course for all. The natural elasticity of his temperament taught Maurice never to despair on his own or on other's account; and he had actually, by this time, brought Philip, and—what was harder still—Philip's familiars, round to a view of the case far from gloomy.

Giving Maurice all the credit for pluck and good intention that he deserves, it must be owned that he had peculiar reasons for feeling cheerful and benevolent at tha tparticular time. The eccentric godfather above-mentioned had shown himself wonderfully tractable and amenable to reason. He had listened graciously to the recital of Dering's matrimonial schemes; and, without actually committing himself, had held out certain vague half-promises of a most satisfactory character. But he stipulated that the engagement should still be kept a profound secret (why—he himself, perhaps, could not have told), and begged that Maurice would not attempt to curtail his leave. This last request was founded on the state of his own health, which was really precarious. The god-son did not think it well to discuss matters over-much; nevertheless he had no notion of obsequious submission. With regard to the engagement, he consented readily that it should not be mentioned to any one except Gascoigne, Chetwynde, and Luttrell.

"There never was but one secret between us," he said to himself, "and I won't make another, if I know it."

He was so firm on this point, that the senior was fain to yield; but he insisted that the wives should not be admitted into the confidence. When Maurice assented to this, it seemed to him a perfectly reasonable condition; beyond this he scarcely thought on the matter.

It might have interested him more, if he could have seen just a little further, backwards and forwards.

The others, with one exception, are much the same as you left them. The lines have grown harder, perhaps, round Chetwynde's braced lips, and his brow is more ready to contract, more slow to unbend, than of old. But dear Aunt Nellie does not look aged by an hour: her face was always rather a sad one; a little of more sorrow or anxiety leaves no traces there. Ida Luttrell meets you—as she met Maurice Dering two days after he landed from India—placid, indifferent, and inscrutable still.

<blockquote>Shall the last ever loveliest be?</blockquote>

says a parlour-poet of no small renown.

Yes, for—in spite of a change that you only begin to appreciate when you have scanned her narrowly—loveliest always is sweet Georgie Gascoigne.

What a change it is, after you do thoroughly realise it! Yet it is rather moral than physical.

It would be hard to single out each detail, or to prove your conclusion by individual instances; but, somehow, you are sensible that Georgie's whole character has seriously deteriorated. Indolence has sunk into lassitude; instead of the timid, coaxing ways that were so charming, you notice a frightened nervousness more painful than pleasant to deal with; the pretty waywardness of a year ago has waxed now into self-will, always obstinate, sometimes passionate.

When Mrs. Gascoigne was first made aware of her husband's state, she betrayed a sorrow and sympathy that, doubtless, were perfectly sincere. She began by being everything that is affectionate and attentive—indeed, up to the present time, she could not be said to have been neglectful of any of her duties—but gradually her temper grew more fitful; she would be impatient and peevish, at times, with others; though with Philip—never. This was especially the case after the inauguration of the London season, when they still abode at Marston.

Gascoigne was not insensible to the change; but it did not surprise him much, or vex him seriously. He thought his pet was naturally dull in the great country house, long void of visitors, and that she missed the social excitement that she had been accustomed to from childhood, and that all her intimates were now enjoying. So he pretended that it would be better for him to be always near his consulting physician, and moved his whole establishment up to their pleasant town house in Park Lane, where Ida Luttrell soon joined them—alone.

Then Philip became very urgent in his endeavours to prevail upon his wife and her cousin to go into society, much as usual. His arguments to this effect were exceedingly ingenious, and palpably sincere. It is not worth while to go through them now: it is enough to say that Georgie yielded, at first with seeming reluctance, afterwards with indifference.

But things did not improve, as the poor invalid had hoped. The more Georgie went out, the more fitful was her humour at home. At last she became subject to violent weeping fits, without any apparent incitement; but of these Philip was, mercifully, kept in ignorance. Her brightest time was immediately after Dering's return. She was unaffectedly glad to see him again: they met, too, without the faintest embarrassment on either side, though they met alone.

All this while, Ida's influence over her cousin grew stronger day by day, till the latter became absolutely helpless in her hands. The self-possession and self-assertion which had stood well by Georgie in many a coquettish *imbroglio*, had utterly deserted her now: she never seemed at ease, unless under the wing of her ally. Sometimes, when the most ordinary conversation was proceeding, she would glance over at Ida in an eager questioning way, as if doubtful whether she had not gone astray in her talk. At such seasons, a very close observer might have noticed Mrs. Luttrell return the telegraph with a strange look, almost impossible to define. It was not reproachful—far less was it menacing. I think I have seen something similar in the grave benevolent eyes of a certain eminent physician, presiding over an aristocratic asylum where everybody is cured by kindness, when one of his patients began to talk—not wildly—but rather too rapidly for decorum.

Still, as was aforesaid—whatever she might be with others—his wife was always tender and gentle with Philip: she never seemed in a hurry to escape from his room, and would break any engagement to sit with him, if he happened to be at all worse than usual, or especially in need of comforting. As for flirtations, she had, apparently, forgotten the meaning of the word. Society, with whom she had always been a favourite, said that "Mrs. Gascoigne behaved beautifully." Did you ever know Society wrong?

So, under the elms, on that August evening, sat very much the same group as might have been assembled under the beeches at Marston Lisle. Others joined them from time to time, and, after lingering awhile, lounged on again: but these it is necessary to weave into the thread of the story in the discourse; on the same principle that has induced me to omit all mention of brothers and sisters and other kinsfolk attached to the actors, who have nothing to do with the *peripeteia* of our piece.

The habits of Spa, as everyone knows, are early, if not simple: to these, in a measure, the Gascoigne party accommodated themselves; dinner was over with them some time ago, though the sun had scarcely set; and round the heads of Dering and Chetwynde thin blue smoke-wreaths were already curling. Hitherto the conversation had been very desultory, and, to us at least, uninteresting.

"By-the-bye," Philip remarked, after rather a long pause, "I wonder what has become of Annesleigh. Has anyone seen him since last night? Those Delaval girls were to have a riding-party, over the hills and far away: I suppose *la belle Diane* has tied him to her bridle-rein."

"I saw him twice to-day," Paul answered, indifferently. "He was at his devotions each time; but he was wooing a female more fickle even than the Delaval 'dasher.' Perhaps he would have succeeded better with the damsel than with the dame; for the dame was— Fortune."

"How fond you are of dark speeches, Mr. Chetwynde," Georgie interrupted, with somewhat of her old petulance. "Wouldn't it have been just as easy to say, that you saw Captain Annesleigh playing and losing heavily?"

Paul shot one of his keen covert glances straight at the fair speaker.

"Just as easy, my dear Mrs. Gascoigne; but

if a humble individual chooses, at rare intervals, to indulge in a small parable, I know no law, human or divine, that forbids it. I was not aware that any one here present was specially interested in Gerald's luck. Besides, I'm not at all sure that he *was* losing heavily: his own face is a bad weather-glass; I only draw my conclusions from poor Penrhyn Bligh's. 'Talk of the ———' I beg all your pardons; but what a wonderful proverb that is. I can't remember having seen it better illustrated."

In very truth, the subject of their talk was just then within fifty yards of them, strolling down the broad walk under the elms, with the indolent grace habitual to him; only now and then you might have heard a small lump of gravel crunched viciously to powder under a grinding heel.

There was a gay smile on the new-comer's handsome lip, as he lifted his cap, saluting the whole group courteously, and subsided into a vacant chair that chanced to be next to Ida Luttrell's.

"How are you, Annesleigh?" Gascoigne said

good-naturedly. "We were just talking about you. I thought you had been a votary of Diana to-day, till Paul said he had seen you—not so profitably employed."

"Paul was quite right—as he always is," Gerald answered with perfect composure. "Not so profitably, certainly; for if I had kept my engagement, I should only have wasted time instead of money. Don't somebody say, they are synonyms? *I* never could find it out. But I'm glad you were talking about me. Perhaps some one will be good enough to administer a slight restorative, in the compassionate line? I'm childish enough still to like it; and look for it, when I'm badly beat."

Ever since Annesleigh's first appearance, the colour had been rising and falling fitfully in Mrs. Gascoigne's cheek; at those last words of his she flushed almost painfully, and leant forward, with eager lips half parted. It so chanced that no one, save her cousin, noticed the impulsive movement. That strange side-glance of warning darted like an electric spark from Ida's phosphorescent eyes, as she too leant forward, so as nearly to screen Georgie's face; and spoke—her own brows contracting.

"Is losing at play the only thing in which monotony does not become wearisome? You will have to go elsewhere for your favourite opiate, soon, Captain Annesleigh, if you draw on our compassion so often and so heavily. It is positively true, that *I* have none to spare to-night. I think you are only punished as you deserve for breaking your engagement to lionise Amblève; to say nothing of your own vow of total abstinence from the tables during this week."

She turned her head imperceptibly, as she threw herself back with a marked impatience; and five words, sliding through her lips, reached only the ear for which they were destined—
" Again, mad—false—and cruel! "

Gerald answered what was spoken aloud, unhesitatingly; and still he smiled his careless, rather defiant smile.

"My dear Mrs. Luttrell, you are incontrovertible, as usual. But let your justice be tempered with mercy. If I have erred, I have suffered; and I shall suffer more before I sleep: for I have yet to make my peace with the great goddess Diana. If she does not resort to *la main forte*, I shall esteem myself luckier than I deserve. Besides, I'm doing vicarious penance for my sins at this moment, in our lodgings; where my poor Pen is casting dust upon his head, and moaning till I don't believe there's a dry eye in the house: even our hard-featured old landlady had melted before I left; and there's a *femme de peine*, extraordinarily fat and foolish, who must be hysterical by this time."

The cloud was not lifted on Ida's brow, and Mrs. Gascoigne's cheek grew paler yet. But though neither Dering nor Chetwynde had any great liking for the speaker, the gay dare-devilry of the man wrung from both more admiration than they would have cared to express: a *really* good loser is so exceptionally rare; they would have wondered yet more, had they known the exact state of Gerald's finances. He left England, with every shilling paid up at The Corner; but Goodwood had drained every available resource to the uttermost drop; luck at play with him, now, was a question of social life or death.

Philip Gascoigne murmured something about "being ready to help, if Annesleigh was really in a scrape." But the other interrupted, before half the sentence was completed—

"Thanks—a thousand times," he said, more earnestly than usual. "It's only too kind of you to offer such things. But, I'm in no such need at present. Perhaps the tide will turn before it leaves my boat quite high and dry. I mean to pull it all back on the September races here: that is, if Dering will ride. We shall have an animal in that will be hard to beat over this country: and we might bring off another *coup*, nearly as good as The Moor's. By-the-bye, Dering, I want to ask your advice about these same races. I won't keep you ten minutes; but I never could talk business in company."

So the two strolled away together.

As Gerald rose, he murmured a few syllables in Ida Luttrell's ear; she bent her head ever so slightly in answer. But through the rest of the evening she was unnaturally grave, and almost absent; also, the cousins held a cabinet-council, for a long hour before they slept.

CHAPTER II.

CONSPIRATORS.

Every sojourner at Spa will remember a certain Temple, perched on the narrow *plateau*, where the zig-zags of one hill-side culminate and converge. It is a very unassuming little fane, of the Early Cremornesque order of architecture; and affords not a pretence of shelter from either wind or sun. Nevertheless, it is rather a central point, and not to be mistaken; therefore, the more convenient for *rendezvous*.

Some time before noon on the following day, Mrs. Luttrell might have been seen, loitering slowly along in this direction; she carried a book in her hand, but had not yet opened its pages; indeed, there was an anxious, worried look on her face, told plainly enough that study was not her object in seeking solitude. Solitude — comparatively speaking — she was sure to find: those tempting woodland walks are almost deserted till late in the afternoon. The active ruralisers urge some of the multitudinous ponies far afield over the *bruyères;* the invalids have exhausted their energies in a matinal toil up to the Fountains; the inveterate *flaneurs* of Pall Mall or the Boulevards stroll complacently down the level *Allée*, without dreaming of breasting the hill.

As Ida neared the Temple, she saw a tall graceful figure leaning against one of the pilasters—a figure that she recognised at the first glance. She had never expected that Annesleigh would miss the appointment; nevertheless, she drew back for a moment, as if in doubt; and ground her white teeth angrily as she at length drew near.

He saluted her very courteously, and cast away the cigar he was smoking before he came to meet her. They turned aside, as if by mutual consent, into a path less frequented than the rest, which skirted the wood, and led on over the heath, ascending still into wilder forest-ground. For some seconds they walked on in silence: Ida spoke first.

"I did not like to refuse to meet you. But I scarcely know why I have come. I fear I cannot help you any more. How could you be so mad yesterday—and after all you promised?"

Gerald laughed—a low, musical laugh, yet not a pleasant one.

"You, who have read so much, must have read about 'dicers' oaths.' When I broke mine, yesterday, I thought perjury would have paid itself by a succession of *séries*. I won't trouble you with a detail of deals; but indeed I had won a good stake twice;—once almost enough to have squared all accounts here. I'm glad you don't say, 'Why didn't you stop?' *You* know, as well as I do, why I didn't do so; but many women would have asked the question, notwithstanding. You can't help me any more? I'm sorry for that; but try and think a little. I'm sure you would, if you could."

A coward—had he been ever such a villain—would have shrunk from the dark glance of hatred that escaped from under Ida Luttrell's eye-lashes. But Gerald Annesleigh never knew what fear meant; and, moreover, had confronted, in his time, every phase of woman's passion.

"I would help you if I could," she said between her teeth. "You think so—while you keep those fatal letters of mine. You are partly right; yet only partly. Fail in your part of our compact—and see how long your hold on me will last. But you have played your game fairly—so far,—it is *your* game, remember, and has always been, though I have backed you. I will try my uttermost to serve you now. I'll go to the bankers and see if they will let me have some thousands of francs without drawing at once on England. I don't think they will refuse, especially as Philip Gascoigne has so large a credit there. I like you better for not taking his money last night; perhaps you will win all back before Geoffrey comes to fetch me (she never shivered as she spoke that name); if not, I must tell him I have been playing, or have made you play for me; or—whatever lie comes uppermost. Let that pass; it is my concern, not yours. I think I can help you this once;

but remember—lose or win—this is the very last time."

Gerald looked steadily in her face, and saw that she meant every word; but his thanks were not the less warmly expressed. Thenceforward their talk became more low and earnest, but it shall not all be recorded here, though Georgie Gascoigne's name recurred perpetually. It shall not all be recorded, simply because a more revolting spectacle than a deliberate seducer, is a woman aiding and abetting her sister's dishonour.

"And you've wrung nothing decisive from her yet?" Ida said at length. "There is little time to be lost. If Philip Gascoigne is helpless and unsuspicious, his friends may be neither one nor the other. I believe they would not hesitate at crime, sooner than see him wronged."

Gerald Annesleigh laughed out loud. To speak the truth—base and depraved as he was—the calm cynicism of his female confederate had had rather a depressing effect upon him, during the last quarter of an hour. It was quite a relief, to hear of a prospect of physical danger.

"His friends?" he said, carelessly—"they're only men, and don't count. I wish one could defy the women as safely. I'm more afraid of those green eyes of the Czernikoff, than of all the others in Spa put together. She owes me an old grudge; and those are the only debts she ever pays. Not hesitate at crime? Legalised murder, I suppose you mean: that's the last nickname for duelling. Well, I shouldn't mind exchanging shots with Paul Chetwynde. But I'd rather shirk Dering if I could; not because he's the most dangerous, but because—What's the matter, Mrs. Luttrell?"

He might well ask the question.

In place of the cool conspiratress, who for the last half-hour had been plotting and planning at his side, there stood a passionate woman trembling in every limb; her face unnaturally white, like steel heated sevenfold; her black eyes blazing with implacable menace and wrath. As she spoke, almost in a whisper, she clutched his arm with her slender fingers till he fairly shrank from the pain.

"You—you meet Maurice Dering—and for

her sake? You had better cut your right hand off than lift it against him. You know something of what I am capable when I hate: if you harmed Maurice, you should know —*all!*"

Anneslcigh was rather startled at first, by the intense passion that he had unintentionally provoked. But he recovered himself almost instantly, feeling rather ashamed of the momentary weakness; he extricated his wrist from Ida's grasp, gently but very decidedly; and there was an inflection of sarcasm, scarcely suppressed, in his voice, as he answered,

"My dear Mrs. Luttrell, it is never remunerative to be over-hasty. If you had only allowed me to finish my sentence, you might have spared yourself all that excitement. You would have heard, that I'd rather shirk Dering—not because he's the most dangerous, but because I like him: though, I might have added, I doubt if the feeling is reciprocated. Are you satisfied now?"

Ida's self-possession returned, but less quickly than her companion's. Before he had finished speaking, she was walking on by his side just as composedly as ever. If she guessed that she had betrayed another of her secrets to Gerald, it is certain that she was conscious of no fresh shame; she was strong in the calmness of desperation there. *He,* at least, could think no worse of her, than he was bound to think already.

"Yes, I am satisfied," she said, with her wonted deliberation. "I was too foolish to take alarm at all. With the commonest caution, there need be no danger from any quarter. We will separate here, if you please. You shall hear what I have done at dinner. That will be soon enough."

Gerald's salute at parting was as courteous as it had been at meeting; but, as he wended his own way home through the forest paths, his musings broke out aloud, rather incoherently, through the smoke of a fresh cigar.

"Did anybody ever see such a born *diablesse?* I thought I was up to a thing or two; but sometimes she makes me feel like a school-boy. Ah, *signora,* you have let another mouse out of the trap this morning. I knew how you hated your fair cousin; but I never guessed how you loved Maurice Dering. That rather complicates the question; only, I really believe, there's no chance of a row. The odd thing is, that all this encouragement—and substantial help, too —is given me, when I wanted no encouraging. I've set my heart on winning that delicious little creature ever since I first set eyes on her. I shall be in clover when the old man dies, and I don't see why I shouldn't make her happy enough, if she can stand the *esclandre*. I can't well fail now, especially with such a backer as I've got. I've a sort of idea, that Ida must exactly resemble a certain Countess of Shrewsbury of unblessed memory. I feel certain that she'll beat the banker; and I've no scruple in borrowing from *her*, though I wouldn't touch Gascoigne's money."

Now, though all this was coarsely expressed (as was Gerald's wont when he soliloquised), it was, perhaps, neither unfair nor untrue.

Yet these last words were spoken of one who had wedded into a family, on whose honour no stain had rested for centuries,—of the wife of one of the most honest and simple-hearted men that ever breathed God's air,—of a woman who, if physical innocence was the sole test of purity, might have cast the first stone at an adulteress brought to judgment.

CHAPTER VI.

ON THE VERY VERGE.

The second evening after these things were said and done, there were great doings at the Géronstère. The paternal Administration called the entertainment, a Grand Feast of the Children; but in point of fact, those innocents were very much in the minority (as they invariably are at Spa), and, after night set in, did not greatly intermeddle with the pastimes of their elders.

It was a picturesque scene altogether, in spite of a certain tawdry flimsiness of decoration. It was pretty to watch the many-coloured chains of lamp-jewels streaming away, in all directions, from the central blaze, through dim forest-paths, till their last faint sparkles merged in the outer darkness. Most of the celebrities of the place were there, gorgeously or tastefully apparelled, each leading her string of willing captives, and keenly alert for fresh live-booty.

Helène de Lauragais had thrown state-craft to the winds, for that one night, and meant amusing herself in earnest; to which end she had bestowed intense consideration on her engagement-card, till each valse and mazurka was parcelled out with a scientific regard to the capabilities of her cavaliers, and her own powers of endurance.

The Czernikoff had not put in an appearance yet. Few marvelled at her absence, for her caprices were proverbial. But—

"*Elle porte donc toujours ton deuil, cette pauvre Princesse?*" murmured the plaintive Polonaise, in the ear of her latest favourite.

The Gascoigne party—excepting Philip, of course—were all present. There, too, was Gerald Annesleigh, looking superbly handsome, and radiant with good spirits. Even the Lichnöffsky was compelled to admit to herself, with an injured sigh, that the palm of masculine beauty could not, that night, be fairly conceded to her own Magyar.

Almost up to the moment of starting, Georgie Gascoigne had professed uncertainty as to whether she would go or remain at home with Philip. It was only to his earnest entreaties that she appeared at last to yield, rather unwillingly. However, when she once got fairly launched into the bustle of the *fête*, her wayward humour changed, and she threw herself into the spirit of the scene with more *verve* and gaiety than she had often shown of late.

The evening was far spent when Paul Chetwynde (who never danced) stood alone, just without the circle of the platform lights, watching a brilliant mazurka in which only the cream of the cream ventured to mingle. Suddenly a tiny hand was laid on his arm, and a low *traînante* voice whispered in his ear—

"A pretty spectacle, M. Chetwynde, is it not? But I would see *all* the wonders of the Géronstère to-night. Will you be my cavalier for a little while?"

The Princess Czernikoff spoke perfectly good English, with a slight foreign accent, and an occasional peculiarity of idiom. Was any civilised language strange to that wonderful woman? Nay; I think, if she had taken it into her head to bewitch a Japanese ambassador, or a Black-foot brave, she would have uttered the charm in their own barbaric tongue.

She and Paul were old acquaintances—nothing more. They met always with mutual satisfaction; and parted without a semblance of regret. For the last dozen years Chetwynde had amused himself with watching the Princess's intrigues, from a disinterested distance; while his cool causticity was very agreeable to the fair Russian's mental palate, on which most conversational delicacies had begun to pall.

So he was quite ready, now, to follow whithersoever she should choose to lead; and they strolled slowly away; turning down—by chance, as it seemed—into the first vista of coloured lights that led forest-ward.

Before they had walked many yards, the Princess made her companion understand—she had mysterious ways of conveying her will, without putting it into words—that she was not, just then, inclined to talk, or be talked to. Paul never forced conversation at any time; so he was quite content to humour her now.

They had nearly reached the end of the walk, where the lamps terminated abruptly, when a significant pressure on Chetwynde's arm admonished him to turn into a side alley winding to the right, which almost immediately divided into two still narrower branches—neither of them lighted.

Paul felt certain he had been brought hither for some purpose: nevertheless, when he heard a murmur of voices through the dense foliage in the paths that, for a short distance, ran almost parallel to that which his companion had chosen, a natural contempt of eaves-dropping overcame all curiosity; he half-faced to the rear, evidently intending to withdraw.

But those lithe slender fingers tightened their grasp, earnestly, on his arm; he heard a faint whisper—less beseeching than warning—"Wait, I pray you, wait"—and looking down, he saw the glimmer of the feline eyes, as they shot evil glances through the darkness.

Three seconds later, Paul could no more have stirred than if his feet had been nailed to the ground where he stood: the blood rushed back to his heart, as it had never done but once before—when he was told, suddenly, of his mother's death. For he heard these words murmured, between sobs, by a voice he knew right well—

"Ah, Gerald—have mercy. How can you press me so cruelly?"

It was Gascoigne's wife who spoke. And at that very moment, Philip was sitting alone; quite happy in recollecting how his arguments in favour of the *fête* had prevailed, and in fancying how his pet was enjoying her evening.

The answer came in Annesleigh's rich mellow tones; and Chetwynde felt his quiet companion shiver ever so slightly.

"Sweetest, I would not be unreasonable for worlds—much less cruel. But I have hoped and feared and waited too long: I *will* have something real to rest upon. This must end one way or the other—and soon. After all, it rests with you to say—'Go.' Then I will never trouble you again after to-night. Many women would think that promise worthless. But *you* know better. You know, that you may trust the broken-down *vaurien's* word."

The bitter sincerity of those last words could scarcely have been assumed. Paul Chetwynde, thinking over these things in the after-time, in despite of his hatred of the speaker, could not bring himself to believe that he was acting just then. The love of a man like Annesleigh is always tinged with selfishness and tainted with intent of dishonour; but the passion is sometimes strong enough in itself to need no deliberate falsehood to back it. Though Gerald felt that poor Georgie Gascoigne was most unlikely to accept the alternative he had just proposed, it is possible that he believed himself honest, in giving her that last chance. Nevertheless, he had played his evil game too often and too long not to know, when the odds were so overwhelmingly in his favour, that he could well afford to be generous.

Something else, too, he knew.

Many women—not over cold or calculating

—looking at his ruined fortunes and wicked notoriety, would have shrunk from compromising themselves, irretrievably, with the incurable Bohemian: for such a step involved, not only sin, but a shame with which Europe would ring. But the thought of this, only drew Georgie Gascoigne closer to his side. The romance that had sprung up, years ago, in her girl's heart, had slumbered for a while but had never died; and of late it had waked again in perilous earnest. She had deluded herself into believing all the rest of the world hard and ungenerous, because it refused to pity or sympathise with Gerald in his misfortunes; and she grew reckless in her wish to make him all possible amends. In spite of her miserable folly and guilty imprudence, it was not really love that she felt for her tempter. With the compassion of which I have just spoken, there mingled a sort of fatal fascination, while she was under the glamour of his eyes, which, in soberer moments of solitude, she was still strong enough to remember with scorn. But the spell held her fast, just now; and when she spoke again, her voice betrayed more plainly the gathering tears. Yet, still she tried to escape from the cruel strait into which Gerald strove to force her.

"Why will you speak of yourself so? It kills me to hear you talk lightly of your troubles, when you will not let me help you—as I would, and could."

"You are a child still, darling," Annesleigh murmured low, in his softest tone—yet not one of his listeners lost a syllable. "Don't you remember that afternoon at Torquay, when you first heard that I was a hunted man? You brought me a tiny purse, with all your quarter's allowance in it, and wanted me to borrow. I took the purse; and I have kept it; but I gave back the sovereigns. So it shall be, now. I will accept nothing from you, but—what I have asked hitherto in vain. And this night shall decide whether you will give all—or none."

It was Paul Chetwynde who was trembling now—trembling till the leaves around him rustled, and the hand, still on his arm, tightened its grasp warningly. In spite of his natural coolness and acquired habits of self-restraint, he could scarcely refrain from breaking in on the interview. For two reasons he forbore: first, because he felt that any *esclandre* in such a place would damage Georgie's reputation irretrievably; secondly, because it was necessary that he should know how far her infatuation would carry her: he still believed that it would stop short of guilt. So he forced himself to listen, quietly, to the low broken words that came next.

"Have you no mercy? Will you not spare? If it were only my own sin and shame, perhaps—— But there is Philip, so kind and trusting and helpless; and my poor little Cecil——"

The piteous agony of her pleading might have moved Belial himself to relenting, if not to remorse: nay, it made even Gerald Annesleigh waver. But he was as ruthless in self-gratification, when his passions were fairly roused, as Machiavelli may have been in statecraft: besides, he had listened, unheedingly, to like appeals

H 2

before—if not quite so earnest—and had made a mock at them afterwards in the midst of his wicked triumph: he fancied, too, the cold scorn of Ida Luttrell's eyes, when she should hear that he had thrown his weapons down when the day was so nearly won. The reaction from the momentary weakness—as *he* would have called it—made him more stubborn than ever; and he spoke sullenly, if not threateningly.

"You ought to have thought of all that before; yes; before you made me, or let me—it's much the same thing—love you desperately. It's too late to ask me to be generous, now. You can answer as you please; but you *shall* answer, at once. I'm not afraid of your breaking your word. Will you promise to be mine; or do we part here—for ever?"

As I said before, fear had much to do with the fascination that Gerald exercised over his intended victim. If Georgie had had any set purpose or plan of resistance, she would never have remembered it then: in a vague helpless terror she felt that the toils were closing round her, and that there was no escape. Almost mechanically, the words broke from her quivering lips—

"Give me time—only a little time."

Gerald saw that it would not do to push intimidation too far; his companion was getting so nervous that she might at any moment become hysterical; and of all earthly things he detested ' a scene ' the most cordially.

"Darling—perhaps I have been too hasty," he said in his gentlest tone. "I have had so much to make me desperate of late, you know. See now: I will be patient for forty-eight whole hours. Then you shall answer me once for all; and, meanwhile, I will not say one word that all the world might not hear. Don't think me a worse savage than I am: I would not frighten you into anything."

Georgie was so weak and helpless and weary, that she could only murmur some incoherent syllables of gratitude, without realising their meaning. Then she began to beg and pray that Gerald would take her back to the others instantly—instantly; she was sure they had missed her already.

Common prudence told Annesleigh that risk enough had been run, for that night: so he made no demur; and only tried to soothe her into composure, with low soft words of endearment. Just before they emerged into the light of the broader alley, Gerald stooped suddenly, and would have kissed his companion's forehead. But she drew back, so quickly, that the lips never brushed her brow, murmuring:

"Not yet—ah! not yet."

It was well for her that so much of prudence and self-respect remained; for if the caress had been completed, it is probable that the cup of Chetwynde's patience would fairly have overflowed. As it was, he remained perfectly mute and motionless, till that other pair had turned a corner of the path that hid them from sight: then he breathed hard and deep, as divers do, after a lengthened plunge, and spoke—still in a suppressed voice, though they were quite alone.

"Your object in bringing me here?"

"You cannot guess?" said the Russian—calmly, but *so* bitterly. "Yet I gave you credit for more penetration than the rest. Did you think I pitied that pretty puppet with the golden hair? I tell you, I would not have stirred a finger to save her. My interest is in that charming compatriot of yours—the man who trades on his fair face, and bright false eyes, and soft lying voice, as merchants trade on their capital. He plays on the folly of us women, like a *boursicotier* on *la hausse et la baisse*. *Il s'imagina de m'exploiter* in Paris, the winter that is past. Do you begin, now, to understand?"

In the midst of his trouble, sprang to Paul Chetwynde's lips the familiar sarcasm.

"Pardon, Princess. I was not so dull as to impute to you disinterested kindness. You would have scorned such a weakness, I know, in the year of your 'first communion.' I did, partly, guess the truth; but it would have been insolence to affect certainty. So you, too, have a debt against Gerald Annesleigh? Be comforted: I think all his scores will be paid, ere long; it is full time."

"A debt?" she said. "Yes—but you know not how deep a one. Listen. I do not tell you how our *liaison* began: this is how it ended.

One night he had lost more than he could pay—apparently he always loses now. He came to me in his distress and I thanked him for so coming; I thanked him, on my knees. I had not enough at my bankers; but, the next morning, I pledged my diamond *suite*—you remember it—the gift of my Empress, and brought him the money before noon. He blessed me, and called me his 'angel and saviour.' Even then, he was betraying me. My rival was a *coryphée* of the *Académie*. At times he will indulge in an unprofitable intrigue. The following week all my letters—the letters that he swore were burned—came back to me. On the envelope was scrawled, in a vulgar feminine hand, '*Avec les complimens sympatiques de Mdlle. Cerisette.*' I do not know that he was privy to the insult; nay, I think he feared the consequences, for he quitted Paris soon and suddenly—deserting his last fancy as he had deserted me. Am I therefore to forgive it? *He* does not so calculate. We meet—as you have seen us; and no word relating to our past has been spoken. But, if Gerald Annesleigh knows how to fear, it is when our glances cross. All these months I have waited; for I would not risk an incomplete vengeance. I believe the hour has come. Is it so, or have I misjudged you?"

While she was speaking, they had moved gradually back, out of the deep shadow, into the lighted *Allée*. It seemed as though the haughty, impenitent sinner cared not that darkness should cover the avowal of her sin and shame. Her wicked glittering eyes gazed up eagerly in her companion's face; they read an answer there before he spoke.

Paul Chetwynde's countenance could be stern and pitiless enough at times, but no living man had seen it as it was now—set, like a steel-mask, in pale implacable resolve.

"You have not misjudged me," he said, speaking low, through his teeth; "and you have chosen your time right well; your patience is likely to be rewarded. Nothing is certain—not even retribution; but I do believe that yonder scoundrel's reckoning-day has come, unless the devil takes unusual care of his own. And, Princess, I care nothing for your motives.

I shall thank you while I live, and will always serve you when I can, for what you have done this night."

"I need no thanks," she murmured; "and,—if I have been wise in waiting,—the end will show."

Her manner and tone very much resembled those of a modest philanthropist, who has just performed a benevolent action, and wishes to escape from gratitude.

They mingled with the crowd round the *parquet*, and separated immediately afterwards, without another word on what they had seen.

Annesleigh had disappeared; and Mrs. Gascoigne was sitting by her cousin, looking strangely white and weary. Paul was not surprised at hearing her whisper, a few minutes later,

"Ida, darling, would you mind going home now? This is not very amusing; and my head is aching so."

Mrs. Luttrell assented readily; perhaps she was only too anxious to be alone with Georgie: her keen eyes had seen, long ago, that a decisive blow had been struck that night; and she had not misunderstood Gerald's covert smile.

Chetwynde and Dering placed the fair dames safely in their carriage; but when the latter was going to take his seat therein, as a matter of course, Paul interfered——

"Ida, I think the road is safe enough for you to dispense with an escort home. I want Maurice, particularly, to walk home with me."

So it was arranged, without any demur or difficulty.

CHAPTER VII.

JUDGMENT.

As the carriage drove off, Maurice turned quickly round: he guessed at once that something evil was in the wind; and the gloom on Chetwynde's brow did not tend to reassure him.

"What is it, old man?" he said. "Let us have it out—and quickly."

The other did not tax his patience long; before they had walked half-a-mile Dering knew all that it was necessary he should know. It would be difficult to exaggerate his astonishment and anger. Giving Georgie Gascoigne credit for much frivolity and a little recklessness, he had never imagined the possibility of her coming within the shadow of dishonour. Treachery to Philip—so utterly trustful and helpless—seemed to Maurice almost too shameful for belief. Yet belief was forced upon him; for he knew that

Chetwynde's evidence was only too convincing and clear.

Cool and determined as he was in all emergencies, he could, at first, not quite collect his thoughts.

"What is to be done?" he said, rather vaguely and dreamily, as if he were speaking to himself.

The answer came, instantly, brief and stern:

"Gerald Annesleigh must die."

Dering never shrank or started; he only listened earnestly while Paul went on.

"Yes, half-measures are worse than useless here. If one were to carry off that poor pretty fool to the end of the earth, she would never be safe from *him*. It would only be putting off the evil day a little longer. Don't I know that devil well; how he will override every law of God and man, if it stands between him and his desire? You could no more check him, now, than you could stop a hound running at view. There's no chance for her while he is aboveground. It can be no heavy crime to rid society of such an enemy: if it be, we must risk it. I wish I could take more than my share of the guilt."

"You are right," Maurice said. "It's a case where one must act rather by the light of nature, than by any written laws. It's no use shutting our eyes to it, Paul; the divines would be all against us here. But I, too, say—we must risk it, and trust to Heaven's mercy for the rest. There will be no need to draw lots about who is to strike the blow. It must be me, of course."

He spoke very gravely and steadily; and his brow was clouded rather with sadness than with anger.

"I fear so," Chetwynde answered, with something like a smothered groan. "I'm no use with the pistols; and your practice is perfect, unless your hand has lost its cunning in India."

"Lost!" Maurice said, with a short, hard laugh. "You would be surprised to see, how much it has gained. When I was getting better, I used to sit under Drummond's verandah, for hours, shooting at all sorts of marks. I got to real feats at last. We shall fight à la barrière, I suppose. If Annesleigh does not shoot first—and straight—I tell you his chance is no better, now, than if he were lying in Newgate under sentence of death."

A moody satisfaction gleamed through the discontent of Paul Chetwynde's face.

"I like to hear you speak so confidently; but it's no use your blinking the question—I wish *I* could. You run a fearful risk. Gerald Annesleigh has been out three times, and never missed his man; and he'll be more murderous than usual this time. There's not a more ruthless savage alive, when he's thoroughly roused."

"Well, I don't know about that," Maurice answered, slowly and rather reflectively. "There's a risk, of course, and I daresay he won't throw a chance away. But I fancy he's had a sort of liking for me, since he won that big stake on The Moor. I shouldn't wonder if he were to try to disable instead of kill. He has never seen me shoot; and won't guess that I can use my left hand as well as my right. This will make the provocation more difficult; and I never yet picked a quarrel with any one. I hate that part of the work worse than all the rest. But it has to be done. They say, he's quick enough at taking a hint of that sort."

So those two went on discussing a hazard on which two lives depended, with more calmness than many judges display when the Black Cap is donned. This will seem absurdly incredible, if you have not realised the peculiarities of their several characters, as I have tried to portray them. They talked on, long after they reached home, and far into the night; but through this discourse it is not necessary that we should follow. Finally, they decided on something like a definite plan of action; and then went, each to his rest.

Of all those nearly concerned in what the morrow might bring forth—with the exception of Philip, who was still in the bliss of unconsciousness—Dering and Annesleigh slept much the most peacefully. Georgie Gascoigne (who had shared her cousin's room of late) lay trembling and sobbing, till weary exhaustion brought broken slumber: Ida was scarcely less wakeful, though she scarcely spoke or stirred; and Paul Chetwynde's busy brain found no respite, even in his brief troubled dreams.

But, if Dering rested well, his waking was not so enviable; for nothing is more disagreeable than opening one's eyes with the consciousness of uncongenial work before one. This was certainly the case with Maurice; and he spent the whole of the day in a state of complete discomfort. Anything like unprovoked quarrelling was so entirely out of his line, that he was fairly puzzled how to set about it. Indeed, chance, rather than design, accomplished late in the evening the desired end.

Annesleigh had spent all the afternoon squiring 'those Delaval girls,' with one of whom he had carried on a running-fight of flirtation for some time past. He appeared in the Redoute soon after dark; and began playing almost immediately. At first he won; but finally a fatal zig-zag of colours came, setting all *tableaux* and calculations at nought, which brought most of the deep players to the very end of their resources. Curiously enough, just at the beginning of the intermittences, Gerald chanced to look up, and caught Maurice Dering's eye fixing him from the opposite side of the table. Like all thorough-paced gamblers, Annesleigh was superstitious in a certain way: he believed in Luck, just as implicitly as he disbelieved in Revealed Religion. He could not get rid of an idea, that that steady gaze was inimical to him; or, at least, had somewhat to do with his evil fortune. More than once, he half rose from his seat, meaning to speak to Maurice; but a fear of ridicule held him back. Ere long, the decisive *coup* came: Gerald had not a gold piece left to stake. He never moved a muscle, nor did he betray annoyance, even by a frown: yet he was nearer absolute ruin—and he knew it—than he had been for many a day. Still he was savagely bent on fighting on, so long as he could find one shot to fire. Looking round—coolly and warily, as a strategist might, in sore need of reinforcements—his eyes lighted on a man, standing close to Dering; this man had also been playing and losing, though not heavily.

Lord Carisbrooke was very young, remarkably good-tempered, good-natured, and good-looking; indeed, barring a slight hereditary propensity to drink, few sub-lieutenants of horse are so 'well-conditioned.'

Annesleigh had the true instinct of the Bohemian borrower: he could tell, at a glance, whether a person was likely to 'part' freely: he guessed this to be a safe 'draw.' So, he walked quietly round to where Carisbrooke stood; and, drawing him a little aside, asked for the loan of "a hundred Napoleons, or so:" very much as he would have asked for a light to his cigar. Though the other's revenue by no means kept pace with his profuse expenditure—in truth, his budget at the year's end might have given the great Chase a lesson in financial audacity—it is certain that he would have consented, now, readily; simply from a constitutional incapacity of saying 'No,' without due preparation. But, before he could speak, Dering, standing by his shoulder, spoke curtly and sternly.

"Don't do anything of the sort, Carisbrooke.

You've lost enough for one night, without throwing more money away."

The insult was so direct and sudden, that Annesleigh could not suppress a slight start; but he answered it in his silkiest tone.

"Carisbrooke, I can't congratulate you on the manners of your Mentor. Captain Dering, you imply that I wish to borrow, without the means or intention of repaying?"

"Clearly, I do," Maurice said. "At least, I'm not certain about the means; I *am*, about the intention."

A dim suspicion of the truth dawned upon Annesleigh, as Ida Luttrell's warning came across his memory. His glance at Dering was so keen and significant, that the latter felt himself flush under it.

"We had better finish this pleasant discussion elsewhere—if we finish it at all. But I fancy you've said enough for *your* purpose, already. Carisbrooke, thanks all the same: I know you were going to part with that hundred. Perhaps it's as well as it is; that money might only have followed my own. *Au revoir*, Captain

Dering:" and so, Gerald lounged listlessly away.

Carisbrooke had not seen much of life yet; of its dark side comparatively nothing. But he guessed that evil deeds were about to be done and was greatly disquieted that through him the offence should have come. Dering stopped his excuses and misgivings at once.

"My dear Carisbrooke, there's no earthly reason why you should blame yourself, or thank me. I interfered, simply because I didn't choose to stand by and see a robbery brought off. I only insist on one thing—that you don't open your lips to any one on the subject, till I give you leave. I think you owe me that much, for saving your hundred."

The other gave the promise, but rather reluctantly. He played no more that night, nor for many a night after; and his solitary cigar, as he walked up and down the deserted *Allée*, musing gravely for the first time in his life, smoked strangely bitter and tasteless.

It is no light matter that will distract the attention of the *galerie* when heavy play is proceeding: in the conversation just recorded, not a tone had been raised in anger; so, what looked like a 'very pretty quarrel,' still remained a secret to all but the principals.

Dering found Chetwynde in another part of the Redoute. As soon as their eyes met, the latter rose and followed Maurice down-stairs: neither spoke till they were in the open air. Then Dering drew a long breath, very like a sigh.

"It's all settled, Paul; or will be, tonight. He deserves all he'll get, no doubt; but—I wish I didn't feel so very like a *spadassin.*

"I know what you mean, right well," the other answered, rather sadly. "It's an evil business, look at it how you will; but—once more—I'm more guilty than you, if guilt there be. How did it happen?"

Maurice told him, as briefly as possible.

"Do you know," he went on, "I'm certain Annesleigh guessed the truth, and saw through that pretext for a quarrel, at once. If so—to give the devil his due—he behaved perfectly. I believe we are not more anxious than he is, to keep Georgie's name out of the whole affair."

"I dare say it is so," Chetwynde said, with a touch of his old sarcasm. "Gerald Annesleigh has the knack of doing a black deed more gracefully than any living man. If he committed a murder, the victim would testify to his courtesy with the last breath. If you had seen him harden himself against that poor child's prayer for mercy—as I did—you wouldn't give him credit for much human-kindness or forbearance. We had better go home now: some one will come on his part before long, depend upon it."

Indeed, they had not long to wait.

Before Annesleigh left the Redoute he had found and commissioned his second. It was no other than the Baron von Rosendahl, of terrible renown; who had been 'out' about as often as Bussy d'Amboise, and was an authority throughout Europe on the minutest points of duel-law. This eminent person soon presented himself at Dering's lodgings; and then and there, with due decorum and solemnity, arranged with Chetwynde the preliminaries of a meeting, to take place early the next morning, just across the Prussian frontier.

When Annesleigh had given instructions to his second—they were very simple and concise—he walked quietly to his hotel, where Penrhyn Bligh sate solitarily over scarcely-watered cognac. Gerald had fancied, of late, that the white anxious face of his *umbra* brought him ill luck at play, and had forbidden his attendance on such occasions. So the poor little creature—for whom society, viewed otherwise than as a source of profit, had no charms—was fain to content himself with hearing of the chances and changes of the cards; that is, if his senses were not wandering on his patron's return.

Bligh looked eagerly into Gerald's eyes, as the latter entered; but they told no tales even to him. He sate down; and, filling a goblet with his wonted deliberation, drained a deep draught of cognac and water, very slowly, evidently relishing it.

"I fear you've lost again," Penrhyn said, at ast, more timidly than usual; for, watching closer, he marked a dark set look on the other's face, that he had seldom, if ever, seen there. "How much is it?"

Annesleigh laughed a little low laugh, as he answered.

"Lost? Yes, of course I've lost. But, my Pen, I don't quite know how much it will come to; nor shall I till to-morrow's over. I mean to go to bed early, all the same; and so ought you, if you want to see me through it decently. I've got to fight Maurice Dering soon after daybreak. Von Rosendahl acts for me; I wouldn't trust those hands of yours with loading: it'll come to closeish shooting I fancy, and a few extra grains of powder might spoil all. But you'll go with me to the ground, of course?"

Weak, and wicked, and despicable as he was, few could have looked, then, unmoved, in Penrhyn Bligh's face: it was so piteously eloquent in its grief and terror, that something between remorse and compassion stirred within Gerald Annesleigh's marble heart.

"Cheer up, old man," he said, more kindly than he had spoken for years, "you couldn't be worse if a hanging-match, instead of a fair fight, were coming off. I told Von Rosendahl that we meant *business;* so I know exactly how he'll fix it. He'll put us up back to back at forty paces; we shall wheel at the word, and fire when we like within fifteen paces of advance. The *barrière* always suits me best. I've no idea how Dering shoots —well, probably, as he does most things. Mark this: I don't mean killing, this time. I shall hold my fire till I'm within thirty yards; for I'm not dead-certain beyond that. If he don't shoot and disable me before that, I'll break his pistol-arm as sure as you live. If he wounds me slightly first, I won't try to hit him at all. But you haven't heard how it happened."

Bligh appeared to listen eagerly to the brief recital that followed, but perhaps he scarcely heard a syllable; his eyes were still glazed and fixed in a haggard terror. At last he moaned out, half intelligibly—

" What *will* become of *me ?* "

There was a terrible simplicity in the words that might have made you forget their apparent selfishness. In truth, was it not as sad as shameful to see a rational being, born to free-agency, so helplessly dependent on another; and that other—one like Annesleigh?

When Gerald answered, though he still strove to speak lightly, it was clear the mocking spirit was dead within him for the nonce.

"It would have been a thousand times better for you, if you had never seen me, Pen. But, as it is, I don't see who would look after you and your morals, if anything happened to me. Don't you think of that. It would be *too* hard lines for both of us, if my number were to be wiped out just when the Emperor is breaking fast, and I might do something for you as well as myself. I'm not going to give you any instructions to-night; for you would remember nothing. Yes, you can remember this. In case of the worst, you'll find a letter in my travelling-bag. Do exactly as it tells you. You'll find jewels enough to carry you home, with the few louis you have left. Now, I'm going to send you to bed, after one more glass. I've set my heart on your looking respectable on the ground to-morrow."

Bligh brightened up a little, under the influence of the other's confident manner; but a more dejected and miserable man seldom laid head on pillow. His physical courage was rather below par; but it is certain, that he would have readily taken all the danger on his own frail shoulders.

After Annesleigh had seen Von Rosendahl, and settled all necessary arrangements, and written half-a-dozen letters, he sate, musing, for awhile, more gravely than despondingly. It may be that during that brief interval between recklessness and oblivion, some solemn thoughts may have passed through that wild, wicked heart; regrets too, not utterly wasted, and vague schemes of amendment never to be realised.

Who can tell? Though the probabilities are fearfully on the side of justice, we may not deny that the mercy which smiled on the Thief's death-pang may possibly be extended to those who need it yet more sorely.

CHAPTER VIII.

EXECUTION.

ONE of these quaint little valleys, between steep wooded hills, that one sees only in the Ardennes, where the meadow sward keeps its tender emerald-green long after the upland pastures are parched berry-brown, thanks to the streamlet whose rippling murmur summer heats are powerless to quell—a light breeze rustling through the leaves of dwarf oaks and birches—over all, the clear crystalline atmosphere of an early August morning.

On the narrow strip of level ground between the water and the wood, two men stand back to back, at a distance of forty paces, measured with unerring accuracy by a practised stride: they are the principals, as you may guess, in the barrier-duel that is just about to begin. Somewhat aside, about midway between the two, is a group made up of the seconds, an Austrian army-surgeon, and Penrhyn Bligh.

The Teutonic faces are stolid and passionless, as if they were carved in beech-wood; but Chetwynde's is deathly pale; though its set, steadfast expression contrasts strongly with the nervous agony that convulses Penrhyn's features in a grotesque horror. No word had passed, when Paul led Dering to his station—only a long hand-gripe, during which neither pulse fluttered or trembled.

Look at the two men, as they stand—motionless as statues—waiting for the signal to be given. Their attitude is nearly the same; both right arms are bent back, so that the pistols point upward perpendicularly; but Annesleigh's left is braced athwart his chest, so that the hand supports the other elbow, while Dering's hangs easily at his side. Maurice's lips are more firmly compressed than usual, and the grave composure of his face is perhaps not altogether devoid of anxiety. On Gerald's brow there is not a cloud of concern—much less of apprehension; the musings of last night have left no trace behind; in spite of the incongruity of time and place, surely some pleasant passing thought must provoke that half-smile.

The Baron von Rosendahl had won the toss —his luck on such occasions was supernatural —and was to give the signal. He gave it almost immediately; smiting his hands together, in one sharp abrupt clap, that sounded like wood striking on wood.

The men wheeled, and stepped out forward, exactly at the same instant. As Dering set his foot down on the third pace, he levelled and fired.

Annesleigh halted on the shot, just as a troop-horse halts on the trumpet-call; he stood for a second or more—steady as a rock, only moving his left arm slightly lower on his breast; then he raised his right slowly, still keeping the pistol pointed upwards, so that the barrel stood out in relief against the sky. Paul Chetwynde saw that in hand and weapon there was no more tremor than if they had belonged to a marble effigy: his pulse stopped beating then; for he felt that Maurice's life was at the mercy of one who, in hate, as in love, had never been known to spare.

Annesleigh's voice rang out, through the clear morning, distinct and loud—but there was not one strained note in its music——

"Dering—we're quits at last."

As he spoke, he fired straight upward; and the next instant, without a shiver or a stagger, crashed heavily forward on his face.

The first sound that followed, none that heard it will ever forget—liker the howl of some tortured animal than a shriek of human agony: it broke from the writhen lips of Penrhyn Bligh. Though he swayed and tottered as he ran, he was the first to reach the wounded man's side, and strove vainly to raise him, with powerless shaking hands.

When they turned Gerald over, a thin red stream was trickling sullenly down his left side. The Austrian surgeon shook his head ominously: he had had long practice in bullet-wounds, and detected, at once, fatal internal bleeding.

The handsome face was lividly pale already; but not one of the features was distorted: if it had not been for a slight quivering of the lids, you might have thought that the great dark eyes, half veiled by the trailing lashes, were only weary. The eyes unclosed, however, almost as soon as they raised him: they lighted first on Maurice, who stood by—looking very sad, if not remorseful.

"Stand back—all of you—for two minutes," Gerald said faintly. "I *must* say a dozen words to Dering—you'll hold me up, won't you? It's no use looking at the wound: I knew I was a dead man, directly I was hit. Take Pen away; or don't let him moan so."

They did as they were bidden, though Von Rosendahl frowned gloomy disapprobation of such a violation of duel-punctilio as interchange of confidences between principals. As Dering knelt down, supporting his enemy's head on his shoulder, the cold sensation of blood-guiltiness tightened its hold on his heart.

"You'll believe me,"—Annesleigh went on— "for you can't help it; it can do me no good to lie. Of course we know what was at the bottom of this. She's weak and rash sometimes; but,

I swear, she's as innocent—so far—as my dead mother."

He spoke with a painful effort, hesitating between each word, in a way that letter-press can hardly represent.

"I do believe you," Maurice said, sadly, "and I know she is both weak and rash. To keep her innocent, I have taken your blood on my head. God forgive me! It looks cruelly like murder now."

"You did well," the other murmured. "There need be no malice between us. I always liked you, and I *did* spare you to-day. Ask Pen what I said last night. He'll give you some papers soon: do what you like with them. I believe my last deed is a good one, though it goes against the grain. If you ever feel sorry for this, or think you owe me a turn, give poor old Pen enough to keep him decently: he won't trouble you long. I'm going fast—look here—I'm not a bit afraid; but—I think I'd die easier if you would give me your hand—just once."

The man that would have rejected that petition, would have owned a harder heart than

Maurice Dering's. As the pressure was exchanged, the shadow of his old sweet smile played round Gerald's lips; and his eyes closed for a second or so. When he opened them again the death-film was gathering there fast: it was evident that his ear guided him, as he beckoned feebly to Bligh.

The miserable creature tottered up, and casting himself on his knees, broke out again into sobs and meaningless wailing.

"Hush, Pen," Annesleigh whispered, in a voice barely audible. "Can't you say 'Good-bye' quietly? It's hard, on both of us. I'd have made a man of you again, if I had ever come to my own. I wish I hadn't bullied you so much. I wish—too late—though—too late. Only, remember——"

Here his voice failed utterly; he closed his eyes once more, and the bystanders, except the surgeon, whose finger was on his wrist, thought that all was over. Suddenly the heavy lids stirred and were lifted ever so little; and the lips began to move. Dering, who still supported Gerald's head, leant forward to catch those last faint syllables; slowly they dropped out—one by one—

"How—the—Jews—are—sold!"

As he spoke, his face seemed to light up, for an instant, in a flash of scornful triumph; then a change swept across it, as if a greyish veil had been drawn swiftly down: a slight choking in the throat, and a shiver that was scarcely a struggle, told of the flitting of that wicked wayward soul.

Though Gerald Annesleigh's latest word was a mock, a truer one was never spoken. Considering that nothing politically important was affected, few more costly shots have been fired than that one whose echoes had scarcely ceased to ring. All the insurance policies on the dead man's life were only waste paper, now; for all the colossal sums raised on his reversions, that little lump of lead had given quittance in full. There arose wailing among The Tribes, such as hath not often been heard since the days of the Captivity; and one or two plaintive capitalists still refuse to be comforted.

There was silence for a moment or more

among those who watched the death-pang, only broken by Penrhyn Bligh's suppressed sobbing; for—obedient to the very end—he had crushed down clamorous grief. Chetwynde spoke first.

"We must not linger here. We ought to have been back over the frontier by now; and we can do no good by staying. Yet—I don't like——."

They all knew what he meant. Though Gerald Annesleigh was far beyond human help or harm, it seemed brutally unfeeling to leave him lying there alone. In truth, the strange fascination that had made the dead man so fatal to his kind, still seemed to abide in the sad, solemn face, that rested where Dering had laid it gently down—not a sign of anger or pain marring its unearthly beauty.

But the Baron Von Rosendahl was a very practical person, and case-hardened by murderous experience.

"*Vous avez raison, M. Chetwynde ; il ne faut pas se dévouer pour les morts. En sus, M. Bligh, peut soigner le transport et l'enterrement de son pauvre ami. Il ne risque rien; puisqu'il n'a pas servi en témoin.*"

"He is not fit——," Paul said, laying his hand, mechanically, on the mourner's shoulder, as he knelt, bending over the corpse, his face buried in his hands.

Neither the words nor the gesture were unkindly meant; but they seemed to wake in Penrhyn Bligh the wrathful devil that had slumbered for many a year. No one would have thought that those weak, pale eyes could glare so savagely.

"How dare you touch me?" he said, in a hoarse whisper, "or meddle in *our* concerns? D—n you! You're not satisfied with murdering him; you can't leave me to do as I like with his corpse." The bitter blasphemies that followed are not such as can be written down.

Chetwynde saw that it would be useless to linger: arguing with Bligh in his present state, would have been like trying to convert a maniac. He took Dering's arm, and drew him away, after the Austrians, who had already moved off.

All Maurice's arrangements, providing for a

fatal termination of the duel, had been made over-night. Honourable homicide is a venial crime enough in these parts; nevertheless, for many reasons, he chose not again to present himself in Spa. He went straight to the station—avoiding the main street of the town—where his servant was waiting for him, and travelled direct to England, without stopping on the road. He and Chetwynde talked long and earnestly on their way back; but their converse does not bear materially on the story; so I omit it, just as I forbore to allude to the husbands of the Lichnöffsky or the Lauragais — excellent personages in their way, but, by the world, completely ignored.

When Paul Chetwynde told Princess Czernikoff of that morning's work, she heard him out with a hard smile on her lips, and nodded twice or thrice approvingly at certain points in the story. She was also careful to discover, where the body was likely to have been conveyed.

Twelve hours after Gerald Annesleigh died, there stood by his corpse a stricken, haggard woman, with an awful agony on her livid face, driving her sharp nails into her quivering flesh, cursing herself, that had willed—the hand that had wrought—the God that had permitted the slaughter. Just so, over the wicked Earl, may have raved the miserable avenger, who

>Hated him with the hate of Hell,
>But loved his beauty passing well.

The tidings came upon the Gascoigne party like a thunder-stroke. Even Ida was, for the moment, bewildered by the suddenness of the blow. This soon settled down into a sullen despondency, such as a captive might feel when the iron bar, that has nearly set him free, breaks in the wards of the last lock. Surely, too, her hard heart was not exempt from a dull, vague remorse, as she remembered how, twice or thrice, Gerald Annesleigh had seemed to hesitate in his evil path, as if foreboding whither it would lead; so that, perchance, he might have turned back, had *she* not been near to goad him on to his doom.

It was from her that Georgie learnt the black

news; and she witnessed, alone, the first hysterical outbreak of the poor child's grief and horror. Ida's stern self-possession, and strange influence over her cousin's weaker mind, triumphed at last. None other in the household saw Mrs. Gascoigne till she was comparatively quite composed; her face, then, betrayed no more violent emotion than would be natural to any soft-hearted woman, brought suddenly in contact with a violent death. As was aforesaid, she had never loved Gerald Annesleigh; it was a feeling quite undefinable, originating in absurd romance, and deepening into helpless fascination, not devoid of fear. After the first spasm had past, a certain sensation of freedom and relief possessed her, though she would never have owned it. Surely some feeling of thanksgiving mingled with her prayers of contrition and intercession for the dead man's soul. One remorse she was spared.

With that innocent false-logic, wherein our sisters excel the sophists, she had forced herself to accept Paul Chetwynde's version of the quarrel; and never suspected that her own

honour had been redeemed at the bitter price
of blood. But, though conscience was silent
here, Georgie Gascoigne knew that she had been
saved—once for all. In life, no woman should
need two such warnings. In good truth, the
vow of prudence that she took upon her, that
terrible day, never afterwards was near the
breaking.

Philip was dreadfully shocked and pained.
He was sorry, of course, for Annesleigh, for
whom he had conceived rather a liking of
late; but he was sorrier yet for Dering. Only
yesterday he would have laughed at the idea
of that kindly nature's incurring the burden of
blood-guiltiness, on a pretext apparently so slight
and shallow. He did not judge his friend
hardly, nor like him a whit the less; but he felt
that they never would see again the cheery,
genial Maurice of the old time: on that honest
right hand there ever must abide the one stain,
over which the waters of this world have no
power. Neither could Philip absolve Chetwynde
of criminality, and told him so.

The latter absolutely declined to discuss the

question. When the other, thoroughly mystified, begged at least to know if there were nothing more below the surface of the quarrel, Paul replied,—" That there had been ill-blood for some time past between Dering and Annesleigh; that he wondered Philip had not noticed it; and that natural antipathies were just as good a reason for fighting as any other."

Chetwynde was always especially cynical, when his case was weak. Gascoigne was not convinced; though of the truth, neither then nor later, did he entertain the faintest suspicion.

" I can't argue with you," he said, sorrowfully; " but I know you are bitterly wrong, and so Geoff would tell you. How do you suppose *he* would take this? No; I never noticed anything of that sort—I notice so few things now. I always fancied poor Annesleigh rather liked Maurice. You say, yourself, he fired in the air. Let us get out of this accursed place before night; my dreams would be spectre-ridden here. I'm certain Georgie would wish to go. Poor darling, she's as much shocked and grieved as I am, which is no small word. Something ought to be done to help that unhappy Bligh."

"I've provided for that," Chetwynde answered curtly. "Yes, on all grounds, it is better to move—homeward, of course."

Ten days later the party that you saw sitting under the elms at the *Allée*, sate — sadly diminished and altered—under the beeches of Marston Lisle.

CHAPTER IX.

MISERRIMUS.

In all his life, up to the fortnight immediately ensuing on these events, Maurice Dering had never known what 'low spirits' meant. The depression and self-reproach under which he laboured, was not lightened by a visit from Geoffrey Luttrell. The parson was not unduly harsh or severe; but he spoke very plainly and decisively, not attempting to disguise his abhorrence of the deed that had been done, or his grief on hearing that his friend had so fallen into temptation.

More than once Maurice was tempted to reveal the real cause of the fatal quarrel; but it was not his own secret, and he forbore. So they parted—not in unkindness—yet with the sense of a barrier between them that had never existed till now, and that might be long in vanishing away. Geoffrey was on his way to Marston, where his wife was awaiting him.

Maurice still remained in town, chiefly because a man in his set could find no more solitary sojourn in early September. He did not feel equal to affronting the curiosity of society, as yet; for, though few regrets were wasted on Gerald Annesleigh, his death created a very marked void, and no slight notoriety was certain to attach to his slayer.

One morning Dering was sitting alone, rather more pensive than usual: he had just finished a letter to Alice Leslie, and another to her uncle. He preferred their hearing the truth—or as much of it as he dared to tell—from himself, and without delay. From the first, he had never disguised from himself, that the stain of blood on his hand might make him unworthy again to clasp that other innocent palm, that he had pressed so often and so tenderly. His happiness, not less than his life, was at stake when he faced Annesleigh's pistol.

In both letters he did not dissemble his regret; yet he did not altogether abase himself: he only prayed them to judge him as mercifully as they could—though the *whole* truth he might not tell—and promised to abide by their decision, without murmuring.

The last letter was scarcely finished when there came a weak, wavering knock at the street door: a minute later, Penrhyn Bligh entered.

The sight of that ghastly face and tottering figure, smote Dering with a pang of compunction, sharper than he had yet felt. Instinct told him that his hand had, unwittingly, dealt the finishing stroke to an incomplete ruin. The ship was stranded long ago, but never quite broken up till that last gale.

The frame that had always been spare and thin, was now shrunken and bowed like a man's in extreme old age; the scared eyes kept blinking through their scarlet rims, as if they abhorred the light; the timid chronic smile hovered no longer about the feeble mouth; it was replaced by a convulsive twitching painful to see; and the tremulous fingers would not rest for an instant.

Bligh tossed down a sealed packet on the

table, and spoke in a shrill piping voice—hurrying his words together, as children do who are afraid of forgetting their lesson.

"I ought to have been here before: but—but I couldn't get further than Liège. It knocked me down there. I came as soon as I could stand: indeed 1 did. I hope—I hope I'm in time."

"Don't excite yourself," Maurice said, gently. "And do sit down. I see you have been very ill. What was it?"

Penrhyn laughed a sharp hollow laugh, like a dog's bark. He did not take the offered chair, but stood, swaying to and fro, griping the table with both hands alternately. It was evident that he answered mechanically, and was speaking rather to himself than to Dering.

"What should it be—but the old thing? Only the 'horrors' were worse this time. I never shut my eyes in the dark, now. It's bad enough, by daylight—to be waked by that woman screaming in your ear, just as she screamed the night before we buried him—let alone what you see in your dreams. I wonder if they *are* dreams. I'm getting beat fast: I've got to *fight the snakes alone*, since you shot him."

He stopped abruptly, and began glancing over his shoulder, into one corner of the room, with wild frightened eyes. Something like terror came over Maurice's stout heart: to save his life, he could hardly have spoken just then. He took up the packet, and was just breaking the seal, when Bligh passed swiftly round the table, and clutched his wrist.

"Can't—can't you read?" he whispered, hoarsely; pointing to these words under the address—

"Open this—alone."

Maurice laid the packet down again, with a sigh.

"I can do nothing right, it seems. Now, do take what I am going to say—as I mean it—in kindness. I promised *him*, that I would help you whenever you needed it. You *must* need it now. It would make me much happier if you would let me serve you, in any way."

Penrhyn drew himself together, with a painful effort, and, for a moment, stood up straight and steady: his eyes met Dering's without flinching, and his voice hardly quavered at all.

"Look here," he said. "I'm not proud; and I'm as hard up as man can be. I'd go into a robbery to-morrow, and thank the Devil for being put on. But I'll stand at The Corner, and hold my hat for pence, sooner than take a shilling from you. D——n you: is that plain enough, or shall I make it plainer?"

Maurice shook his head, sadly: he could no more have been angry with the unhappy being before him, than he could have struck an infant in arms.

"Yes, it's plain enough," he said—"plain enough, that I may repent; but can make no amends. I cannot guess what that packet holds; but I thank you for bringing it. Will you let me send you home, at least? You are not fit to go alone."

The momentary ferocity had died out of Penrhyn's face, and the old expression—imbecile when it was not frightened—had returned. He shook his head feebly, as he turned and made his way to the door. Before he reached it, his wandering eyes lighted on a liqueur-case, that stood half-open on a side-table. For a moment or two, it seemed as if he would have resisted the fatal fascination; but it was too strong for him. He staggered up to the table, and poured out a large glass of raw spirit. When he had drained it at a gulp, he broke out into that horrible laugh again.

"I told you I'd take nothing from you," he said. "I was bound to lie; for—I didn't want to have a shaking-fit *here.*"

The door closed behind him, without another word passing; and so Dering was left alone, with the dead man's message before him.

For several seconds he sat, gazing fixedly at the superscription; addressed in the firm flowing hand, that every usurer of note in broad England knew to his cost.

But to Maurice, the handwriting of the letters within the envelope was yet more familiar. He started in displeased surprise as it caught his eye: no wonder—it was Ida Luttrell's. On a slip of paper, Gerald Annesleigh had written—

"Use these or not, as you please. But read them through: there is no treachery in your doing so; I take all that on myself. I hate myself at this moment; but I see no other way of helping that poor woman: she will never be safe while she is in her cousin's power. I have not left one word of leave-taking for *her:* she had best hate my memory. I may be all wrong: but I mean right—for once. Rather late in the day—isn't it? Farewell.

"G. A."

As he read on, the frown darkened on Maurice Dering's brow, till it was black as midnight: he cast down the last letter, with a groan of horror and disgust. There were six, with dates extending nearly two years back; and the proofs were damning beyond possibility of doubt.

Ida had not only been cognisant of Annesleigh's designs on Georgie Gascoigne, but had aided them both by counsel and connivance; she more than once suggested plans for the meeting of those two, and had actually furnished

Gerald with funds to bring him to Spa, besides helping him to pay his play-debts there.

There was a deliberate depravity, and pitiless malice, and shameless cynicism about the whole conspiracy—for such it really was—far beyond what it had ever entered into Maurice's honest heart to conceive. For the moment he felt thoroughly bewildered. It seemed the very wantonness of crime. What earthly object could Ida have in plotting or abetting her cousin's ruin? And how was he to act? He no more thought of keeping Ida's evil secret, than he would of standing by to see felony done. Yet it was impossible to touch her without striking Geoffrey Luttrell to the very heart's core.

With all this misery, doubt, and difficulty, mingled that nervous eagerness to face the worst at once—common to most men of his sanguine temperament. He relied on Chetwynde's judgment far more implicitly than on his own, or that of any other living person. He resolved to seek that counsellor at once.

So a train, early that afternoon, carried

Maurice Dering down to Marston Lisle. He had previously telegraphed to Paul to meet him at the station, about three miles from the house; begging him also to keep his coming a secret from every one.

Chetwynde's disgust and surprise at Maurice's revelations, fully equalled the other's; but these reached their climax when Dering made a clean breast of what had passed between himself and Ida. The vital urgency of the case compelled him to act, just as a criminal does with his advocate—making no half-confessions. During these few minutes Paul's self reliance —not to say self-esteem—sank so many degrees, that it never afterwards fairly recovered itself.

"What a blind idiot I've been all these years," he said, in a low bitter voice; "and I held myself a fair physiognomist and judge of character. Her motives puzzle me still. Wait——. By G—d, I have it. Fancy, not thinking of that sooner. It's as plain as daylight."

Maurice looked inquiringly, and rather wonderingly, at the speaker. After a second, Chetwynde went on.

"Don't you see it? Hate and love were both at work—if you can call that she-devil's passion love. She hated Georgie, because she fancied she had once stood between herself and you; and thought, it might be the same over again. I suppose she gives no man credit for constancy in resistance to temptation. She wanted Georgie ruined, and out of your reach, before you came back. Even if she had not feared that pretty fool, she forgives no more than she forgets. But explanations are not excuses. It's the most infernal case I ever heard of."

"It must be," Dering answered sternly; "for, if you have guessed right, it does not soften me a whit. She don't deserve to be spared."

"Spared!" the other retorted with intense contempt. "She should have short shrift if she alone were to be dealt with. But there's poor Geoff to be considered. I believe, on my conscience, this will go near to killing him."

They consulted long and earnestly, walking through the green by-lanes that led to a side-gate of Marston park. By the time they reached it, they had settled their course of action.

Chetwynde was to go up to the house, and bring Ida to a certain sheltered walk through a remote shrubbery, where Dering was to await them. Paul was to be present at the interview.

It seemed as though some strange fatality hung over the most painful hours of Maurice's life; for once again his nerve and firmness were about to be sorely tried, and—the day was hard upon sun-down.

CHAPTER X.

UNDER THE BEECHES.

CHETWYNDE found Mrs. Luttrell in the garden, alone, for Georgie had hurried back to her husband directly they came in from driving: she had been unusually attentive to Philip of late, and would never leave him for more than an hour or two at a time.

Paul had not patience to invent pretexts: he told Ida, abruptly, that some one was waiting to see her on urgent business, and that she must come with him immediately. The cold sternness of his voice and manner was not to be misunderstood. That vague feeling of insecurity that had haunted Ida ever since Gerald Annesleigh's death became terribly definite, now; but her stubborn spirit rose to the emergency: she followed Chetwynde without demur or objection, and only asked one question,—this was when they were crossing a strip of open paddock between two belts of shrubbery,—

" Won't you tell me who it is ? "

Paul shook his head impatiently : she pressed him no further; and their moody silence was not again broken till they reached the appointed place of meeting.

Dering was leaning against a tree—his head bowed low on his breast—his hat crushed down over his brows so that his face could hardly be discerned : the despondency of his whole attitude would have struck the merest stranger.

At sight of Maurice, Ida felt that her worst fears were more than realised : she had fancied that possibly Penrhyn Bligh might have become possessed of her secret and betrayed it; but she had never dreamed of *this*. Her heart stopped beating for a second or so, and then began throbbing madly; a wild desire possessed her, to fly anywhere rather than be confronted with him; she halted, and had actually half turned round, when Chetwynde, as if he guessed her intent, laid his hand gently, but very firmly, on her arm; she yielded to the impulse without a struggle; but all her marvellous self-command could not repress one low piteous moan.

Dering lifted his head as they drew near: the first glance at his face told Ida that she had scant mercy to hope for. Then she grew stronger, in that awful courage of despair, that has enabled so many weak arms and hearts to hold their own, for awhile, against the heaviest odds. She never shrank or shivered as Maurice came forward to meet them; and her great bright eyes looked into his with a steady earnestness that was neither suppliant nor defiant.

Dering held an open letter in his hand: he held it out to Ida, striking it sharply with his forefinger.

"Do you recognise your own handwriting, Mrs. Luttrell?"

With all the humiliation hanging over her, she was still too proud for useless denials.

"Yes; I wrote it," she said, simply. Having spoken, she drew back a pace or two, and stood, with downcast eyes, and hands locked firmly before her—on her face that pale resolve which is *not* resignation; just as a criminal, who has pleaded 'guilty,' with nothing to urge in extenuation, might wait to hear his sentence read.

"Is it possible"—Maurice said—his voice shaking with passion—"are you made of flesh and blood like ourselves—that you can acknowledge such a letter as this, just as coolly as if it were a note of invitation? Why—I am speaking selfishly now—don't you know that, to stop the plotting which you aided and abetted, I have taken the sin of murder on my soul? For murder it was—call it what name you will,—I see that, plainer and plainer every hour. Of the wrong meditated — aye, and wrought too, against others, I dare not speak or think."

Then Chetwynde's cold measured tones came in: he stood somewhat backward; almost midway between the other two.

"I have the same right as Maurice, to accuse you; for my share of blood-guiltiness is the same. I advised and planned the slaughter; and would have executed it, if I could have trusted my hand and eye, as I could trust his.

But neither he nor I, had—or ought to have had—any special claim on your forbearance. Did you never think of Geoffrey—who never thwarted a whim or quarrelled with a word of yours—who trusts in you as he trusts in God's mercy—when you dragged his honour, and yours, through the mire of Annesleigh's intrigues? Ida—I have known, and liked you, since your childhood; and it has all come to this; that I must speak such words without pity, and you must hear them, without resentment. Ten thousand times over, I would rather have seen you dead."

She looked from one to the other with vague dreamy eyes; and the listless indifference, habitual to her when not much interested in conversation, began to settle down on her face.

"Dead?" she said, softly. "Yes — that would be better. But—as it is—what would you have me do? I make no defence; and I am quite helpless, you see."

In truth, if you could only put the thought of her guilt, for one moment, aside, there would have been a piteous disproportion in the odds: it was cruel, to see that little frail delicate creature matched against those two strong, stern men. When Right is Might, it sometimes hardly obtains undivided sympathy.

"I will tell you what Maurice and I have resolved on," Chetwynde answered. "About sparing you, there has been no thought; about sparing Geoffrey—much. It is clear that your intimacy with Philip Gascoigne's wife must be broken off, at *any* cost. This must be your last visit to Marston. Now, if this can be done, without letting any other person—not even Geoffrey—into this miserable secret—so let it be. There are difficulties and dangers innumerable about it: if any woman living can surmount them, you can. You may use any fair means, and make any fair excuses; but, I warn you, of plots and conspiracies we will have no more. Will you make the trial, on your own risk and resources, or shall the matter be settled abruptly, this night?"

She paused for a few seconds, pondering gravely.

"Yes, I will make the trial—it *is* for Geoffrey's sake, though you will not believe me; yet, it may be only putting off the evil day a very little longer. I can make no promises, even if you would listen to them: but I suppose I shall do my best."

Dering's eyes were cast moodily down, while she was speaking; but Chetwynde's more watchful glance never left Ida's face. From the very first he had failed to detect there one sign of contrition or shame, and this had chafed him sorely; now, he thought he could perceive the glimmer of an unholy hope—the dawning of a wicked triumph. He may possibly have been deceived in the change of Ida's expression; but, a change there certainly was. His own brow—dark enough already—lowered visibly: he set his teeth hard; and, when he spoke, there was undissembled menace in his tone.

"One thing more. You must have noticed that hitherto there has been no question as to your motives in plotting Georgie Gascoigne's ruin. Shall I tell you why I asked you nothing? It was because I know all your shame

—yes—all. I know what grudge in the past lay at the root of your hatred; what temptation in the future led you to combine against her honour. I know——"

She broke in here, with a cry, so piteous and agonised, that it sent a shiver through both her hearers, steeled though they were against relenting.

"Not that," she moaned, "anything but that. Tell everything to Geoffrey—to Philip—to all the world. But, Maurice, you *won't* let him taunt me so, before your face. Ah, how *could* you tell him?"

For the moment the positions of accuser and accused were changed. Maurice felt himself the culprit: those plaintive tones smote upon his conscience as if he had been guilty of base betrayal of confidence. Instinctively his fingers closed upon what they held; the touch of those infamous letters brought back all Dering's firmness; he spoke quite steadily.

"You are right, in this at least. Paul shall not say one other word on that subject. I—but very few. I had hoped those wild fancies were dead long ago. Yet it might have been better you should have known sooner, that, in India, I pledged myself—hand, and heart, and soul—to one whom I love, not better; I think, than she loves me; who will, I hope, ere long be my darling wife."

Late, very late, but fearfully complete. Ida's punishment had come at last.

False wife—false friend—double traitress; she was all that, and more; yet, scarcely any human creature could have forborne from pitying her, as she drank the first bitter drops of retribution. With the death-cry of her wicked love and mad jealousy, mingled the voice of a mocking devil; murmuring that the shame and sin had all been incurred in vain. The piteous pleading vanished from her face, as it hardened like a white flint-stone.

"That woman's name?"

If you never heard Rachel whisper, I can give you no idea of the intonation with which those three words were spoken.

"Her name matters nothing," Maurice said. "And I would no more think of uttering it at such a time as this, than I would tell her one word that has passed here. By God's help, I will keep her clear, even from the knowledge of any sinful or shameful thing."

Now, mark how it stood with Ida Luttrell. She knew that she had fallen to the lowest depth in the estimation of those who were privy to her guilt: she knew that, if she escaped open dishonour in the sight of others who ought to have been yet nearer and dearer to her, it could only be at the price of weary dissimulation and endless invention of pretexts: she knew that, if, after all the scheming, the black secret oozed out, the last state would be worse than the first, for even Geoffrey must, then, needs shrink from her side, if he did not cast her utterly adrift: she knew, too, that the Fiend's arch-juggle had been played over again; the sinner had sold herself for a shadowy bribe, when the real treasure had been given long ago to another. Yet—it was not remorse or shame that was tearing, now, at her heart-strings.

She only thought, of the broad deep gulf that had been opened, that day, between herself and

Maurice Dering—never, while they lived, to be closed again: she would have borne up stubbornly to the very end, if she had not marked the reverent tenderness of his manner and tone, when he spoke of the woman who had won his love. There are limits—as the ancient tormentors could have told—to mere human endurance, physical or moral: at that last turn of the rack, Ida's gave way.

Her whole nature seemed suddenly transformed: her eyes blazed out, with a wild fierce light; her voice vibrated like a chord struck when it is strained to breaking; and her slight frame trembled with passion, till the plumes of her *aigrette* quivered again.

"You will not speak her name? I will learn it, very soon. Maurice Dering—do you know why? You may trample me under your feet, as you will—you may make me a mark for all the world to scorn—and I will worship you to my life's end. But the woman that you love —I *may* hate her, as I *do* hate—with all my heart, and soul, and strength. Whoever she may be—if you change and love another, it will be still the same. I will harm her if I can. And, now—before she can be yours—I pray that death and dishonour may overtake——"

Her utterance was so rapid, that Paul Chetwynde, who would have checked her, as soon as he recovered from his first astonishment, had not time to do so, before Ida stopped abruptly.

And this is why she paused.

She saw a sudden horror sweep across Maurice Dering's face, as he stood fronting her, that she knew was not roused by her own wild, wicked words; his eyes were fixed too on some object behind her. Before she could turn, a voice—utterly strange to her—spoke, close to her shoulder.

"Ida—are you mad, or—am I?"

CHAPTER XI.

ANGINA.

Yes, the voice was utterly strange, not to Ida alone, but to Dering and Chetwynde. Yet all had heard it a thousand times, speaking kindly or cheerily; and to one, it had been, very often, prodigal of tenderness. Nor was the change to be only momentary: the old round jovial ring of Geoffrey Luttrell's voice was dead for ever.

He was returning from shooting, when he saw his wife and Chetwynde cross that open strip of paddock; very naturally he followed them, and came up unperceived, just in time to hear the last few words of Ida's terrible outbreak.

Hard and intrepid as she was, the unhappy woman fairly quailed, when she turned and saw her husband's face. A month of deadly sickness might have worked less ravages there, than those few seconds of agony.

Geoffrey looked from one to the other of the group in a stunned helpless way, when he found his first question unanswered.

"Will no one tell me what this means? Is it my wife that has just been speaking, to the oldest friend I have on earth? Let me have the truth—and quickly. A very little of this will drive me mad."

Ida stood still and silent—looking white and scared, with her left hand pressed tightly to her side. Dering's face was buried in his hands; but Paul Chetwynde, with a vast exertion of will, forced himself to answer.

"My poor Geoffrey! We meant to have spared you this:—indeed—indeed, we did. But it is too late now. You must know all. Your wife has been very guilty."

Luttrell drew himself up—neither haughtily nor wrathfully; but with a firmness not devoid of dignity, such as might become a priest in execution of his duty.

"Then I will hear it from herself," he said. "Whatever her sin may have been, you are not her judges. She shall ask God's pardon first—

then mine. I trust that both may be granted; but—however that may be—I know this: no created being shall stand between me and mine."

As he spoke, his arm went round the pale shrinking woman at his side; and he drew her closer to his heart; fronting those other two with something like defiance.

A revulsion of feeling, strong as sudden, came over Ida Luttrell then. She did, at last, value aright the true, tender, honest heart on which she leant; the old unholy passion gave place, for a moment, to the fresh pure love, as a fiend may fly before an advancing angel; though he never knew it, poor Geoffrey did really attain what he had struggled for so long and patiently; his wife, as she lay then in his embrace, was his very—very own.

"My dear kind darling," she murmured. "I don't deserve——"

A choking catching of the breath; one quick convulsive clutch of the little hands that rested on her husband's arm; a fearful shudder through every nerve in her frame; a change in the delicate pale features—deadly significant, though not one was distorted; a dropping, not a drooping, of the long black eye-lashes——and Ida Luttrell had done with all shame and sorrow and pain on this side of Eternity.

Infinite Mercy did allow to that misguided spirit one moment of contrition, bitter and sincere, before its flitting: but the lips through which the outbreak of guilty passion gushed so freely, were sealed with the first whisper of penitence.

It was known that Ida's father had died of heart-disease; but no one had suspected its existence in her; nor had any dangerous symptoms shown themselves, up to the day when she was stricken down.

For some seconds, not one of the three men realised the truth. It broke first on Geoffrey Luttrell: he closed his eyes like one blinded by a lightning-flash, and sank slowly on one knee—his arm still coiled round the slender waist—staring stupidly down into the quiet white face.

"Don't—don't—you see she's fainted?" he said in a broken grating whisper.

The piteous pleading of his upturned glance belied his words: they saw at once what horrible fear possessed him, and could not contradict it; but tried to render what aid they could in sorrowful silence.

All the three had looked on death before, in more shapes than one; they could not long keep up the semblance of doubt. Geoffrey had begun to shake and totter under his light burden, before Chetwynde drew it gently out of his arms, and laid it down on the grass, a little aside.

Then ensued, perhaps the most terrible spectacle that can meet us on this earth of ours—the sight of a strong man's agony.

Paul and Maurice had really had the best intentions from the first, and thought they had acted wisely, if not well. Did they think so now—looking on the dead woman's lovely face, where the death-smile was just beginning to dawn; while Geoffrey grovelled at their feet, tearing up the grass by handfuls, and crying on God to save him from the madness of despair?

Look to the End. A sound maxim surely: pity it is so hard to practise. For how far into the Future may we hope to pierce with this dim sight of ours? As we walk onward, around us and before us it is cloudy all: if we stray ever so little from the path that led our forefathers aright, it is well, if over the End brood not the 'blackness of Darkness for ever.'

That awful paroxysm lasted not long: when Luttrell raised his face it was almost calm, though traces of the late convulsion still were there. He drew himself over to where the corpse lay, and knelt by its side, signing to the other two to imitate his example. Not one word was spoken; the faces of all the three were buried in their hands, and the prayer of each was known only to his own conscience; but, during those few minutes, I think Paul Chetwynde's heart went up nearer to Heaven than it had done since his boyhood ended.

Geoffrey first uncovered his eyes; he stooped and pressed a long kiss on the cold forehead; and then rose steadily on his feet.

"Maurice Dering," he said, in a deep hollow voice, "we have been fast friends for years, and I would have doubted the Bible's promises, rather than your faith and honour. I do not doubt them now. Yet—do you know what I have just been praying for, with all the strength that is left me? It is, that I may be enabled to forgive you, as a Christian should forgive. My heart may change—perhaps I am mad still—I cannot tell; but, if I feel hereafter as I feel now, our hands never meet again."

Before Maurice could answer, Paul Chetwynde sprang to his feet.

"You *are* mad," he said, sternly, "and even that scarcely excuses you. Trust his faith? You might well do it; and so you will say when you hear all the truth—as you *shall* hear it, when you are fit to listen, whether you will or no. My lips are sealed in this presence,"—he pointed to the corpse—"but the living shall have justice, sooner or later."

Maurice Dering caught the speaker roughly by the wrist.

"How dare you speak so cruelly?" he said, his eyes flashing angrily through the tears that had made them very dim. "Geoffrey, dear old Geoffrey! listen to me—not to him. I may have been miserably misguided; but towards you, and towards *her*, I am innocent; before God—I am innocent. There never was word of mine that you might not have listened to, and if I kept one secret back, it was only for both your sakes. See—I can swear it: I can swear it—thus."

And, kneeling still, he laid his hand, firmly, on the dead woman's heart.

If the spirit that had so lately departed could have returned, but for one brief second—if those pale lips could have uttered but one brief syllable—would testimony to Maurice's truth have been withheld? I trow not. But the trial by Ordeal is long since obsolete; and, even while that ancient superstition prevailed, though the corpse would bleed afresh at the touch of the murderer, it was neutral and obdurate when the innocent made appeal.

But Dering's words carried conviction even to Geoffrey Luttrell's tortured heart and dizzy brain.

"I believe you," he said, gloomily. "And perhaps I shall thank you, some day, when I see things clearer. I can see nothing now, but—this."

As he spoke, he knelt down again, and began to gather up the body of his wife into his arms, so carefully and tenderly, that the hair was not dishevelled as it rested on his shoulder, nor was a fold of the dress disarranged. The others would have helped him; but Geoffrey motioned them impatiently back, muttering—"No one shall touch her, but me." And so he strode slowly away, towards the house; looking neither to the right nor to the left, nor even into the pale face so close to his own; but always straight forward.

Yet—once he did turn his head. Though he looked at the two who were following, it was evident that he was speaking to himself rather than to them.

"She said—'Darling,' before she died."

Those few words would have carried piteous significance, to the merest stranger. They told, plainly enough, of long waiting and watching for love that never came; of checks and disappointments not the less keenly felt, because even to itself the honest heart dissembled its own bitterness, and never waxed weary, or sullen, or cold. Only—at the last, it drank in that one little drop of sympathetic tenderness with a terrible avidity, as cast-aways on tropical seas catch at stray drops of rain.

Not another word was spoken till they reached the house; entering it by a side-door, whence a staircase led straight to the Luttrells' apartments: it so chanced that they met no one by the way. The distance was not long; and, in life, it was a light burden that Geoffrey carried. But there is an awful weight in a soul-less body, that only those who have supported one can comprehend. When Chetwynde got in advance to open that side-door, he was not surprised to see the big drops standing like beads on his friend's forehead, while the veins stood out like strained cordage.

But Luttrell moved on, still steadily, without halting, till he had laid Ida gently down on her own couch; smoothing the pillows and her dress with the same careful tenderness, that he had shown when he lifted her from the grass.

Then he straightened himself up, and gazed steadfastly into the corpse's face. It seemed as if some magnetic attraction there had influence over his own vitality; for, in a few seconds, Geoffrey Luttrell's cheek grew ashen-white; and without an effort to save himself, he fell forward across his dead wife's feet, in a lengthened swoon.

Only Paul Chetwynde was then standing by. Maurice Dering had said nothing of his intentions to the others; but when they entered the house, he drew back, and strode gloomily away, passing out of the demesne unobserved. He returned to town that same evening, and it was many a day before his feet trod again the woodpaths of Marston Lisle.

CHAPTER XII.

DE PROFUNDIS.

On Philip Gascoigne's distress and Georgie's more demonstrative grief, it is not necessary to dwell. It is enough to say, that for Ida Luttrell was made more and bitterer moan than is allotted to many who go stainless, if not sinless, to their graves. For, of a truth, the influence of these model-matrons seems sometimes to terminate with a strange abruptness; the world that did them such reverence while living, honours their obsequies with little beyond decorous regret.

Geoffrey determined at once that his wife should be buried at Minstercombe, and that the funeral should be as private as possible. Chetwynde hesitated long before he asked to be allowed to attend it; but afterwards he was glad he had done so; for Luttrell consented, gratefully. He never seemed to connect Paul in any way with the train of circumstances that had, in all human probability, hastened his unhappy wife's death. Yet he had himself insisted on full explanations, as soon as he was physically able to listen, and all the miserable truth was before him now. He bore it with wonderful fortitude: men of his calibre, especially when natural power of character is backed by strong principle and faith, are often never more reliable than immediately after the one utter break-down that only happens—not twice in a life-time.

That Geoffrey did not dissemble, or even attempt to palliate to himself, the extent of his wife's meditated guilt, is most certain; but, when his idol lay shattered, he would neither himself trample on the fragments, nor allow others to insult them. When Chetwynde —whose treatment of moral maladies was always rather excisive—hinted that Ida's sudden death was not deeply to be regretted, inasmuch as bitter misery to herself and others had so been spared, Luttrell checked him so sternly, that Paul felt quite contrite and humble for the moment, as if he had ventured on unknown ground, where he had no concern; which, indeed, was very much the state of the case.

The night before the funeral procession left Marston, Geoffrey sent to beg Mrs. Gascoigne to visit him in his own rooms, where he had secluded himself since Ida's death, seeing no one but Philip and Chetwynde.

Georgie was dreadfully shocked at the change in his appearance. His face was haggard and drawn; yet it was very grave and calm. Suffering had refined the features, once so bluff and jovial, into a sort of solemn dignity. She partly guessed the purpose for which she had been summoned; for she had not yet been allowed to see her dead cousin. So, indeed, it turned out.

Geoffrey wrung her hand hard when she entered, and without quitting it, or uttering one word, led her into the inner room, where the corpse lay in its open coffin.

A great awe and fear came over Georgie Gascoigne—looking, then, for the first time on death—as she gazed down on the delicately chiselled face—white as the soft lace around it—not much more still and composed that it had often been seen in life; only—what had been listless indifference, was now eternal peace.

Then, in that changed voice of his, Geoffrey spoke.

"You loved her, very dearly?"

He was answered by a deep sob, and by a pressure from the fingers that he held.

"And you thought that she loved *you?* I know you did, or you would never have trusted her so far——"

A flush swept over her pale tear-stained face, and he felt her tremble; but he went on, never heeding.

"Listen,—this is a secret to be kept even from your husband,—she never *did* love you: more than this, she hated you bitterly, and would have helped to do you deadly wrong. Never ask me, why: I could not tell you if I would; I have only strength enough to tell you this; and that strength was only given me after long, long prayer. Now—knowing all this—can you say, after me—'I forgive her, and I trust that

God has forgiven her, with all my heart and soul?'"

Amongst Georgie's many faults bearing of malice certainly was not one. Besides, she really had loved her cousin well, after her own light-minded fashion, though she had begun somewhat to fear her of late: if the meditated wrong had been wrought out to the uttermost, she could never have cherished rancour against the poor senseless clay. It was not doubt, but grief and surprise that kept her silent. But Geoffrey misinterpreted her hesitation.

"Remember—you were children together, and —she died so very young."

His voice, hoarse and deep till now, softened strangely in its pleading.

Georgie Gascoigne wrested her fingers out of Luttrell's grasp, with a passionate energy.

"Do you think I am made of stone or steel?" she said, through her sobs. "God knows how I loved her; and, if she hated me, she could not have been in her right mind. Ida—darling Ida —what had I ever done to deserve it? I don't want to know what wrong you speak of. If I did know, I would still say—what I say now." She repeated Luttrell's very words, low and reverently, as she would have repeated any other prayer; and then laid her lips, without shrinking from the cold, on the brow of the corpse.

A wintry gleam of satisfaction lighted up Geoffrey's worn face: he drew a long deep breath of relief, as he said—

"I pray that, in this world and in the next, you may have your reward for the comfort you have given me this night. Now, come. What I have further to say, shall not be said *here*."

He closed the door carefully behind them, before he spoke again.

"I will be very brief, and deal with you as gently as I may. But, remember; I speak now, not only as an old friend of your husband's, and a true friend of yours, but as God's minister. I know my duties, if hitherto I have been slack in discharging them. I know, that it behoves me to let no means of salvation slip, though I find them in the depth of my own desolation. This past year has laid upon us all heavy burdens;

upon some, almost more than we can bear. I believe, that in the background of the darkest sorrows some sin or shame is to be found. Do *you* not think so? Let your conscience answer me. I need no confession in words."

Before he had finished speaking, Georgie had sunk to her knees, her face buried in her clasped fingers; Geoffrey could hardly catch the broken whisper—

"Ah, spare—spare me. I have repented—indeed I have; and I have tried so hard to be better."

He laid his hand on her bowed head, with a solemn tenderness.

"Do not fear," he said. "What am I that I should judge or condemn you?—I, who every hour have to appeal to Heaven's mercy; for repining is a sin like the rest. Yes, I do believe that you have repented, and that you are striving to make atonement. I absolve you of the past, so far as I may. It is for the future I would warn. You have opportunities of doing good, such as are given to few: you will be held accountable for neglecting no less than for misusing them. You have it in your power still to make Philip very happy; and this you ought to do at any self-sacrifice. I say nothing of Cecil, for you need no prompting to your duties there. Above all things, remember this. Other women, born coquettes like yourself—forgive me, I must needs speak plainly—may indulge their vanity without serious guilt; but when temptation to such folly besets you, you will be worse than reckless, if you forget that, once, only God's great mercy saved you from falling into a pit, at the bottom of which lay dishonour and death. Now, my first and last sermon to you is done; and I have only to say 'Farewell.' I took you *in there* first; because I would not frighten you into saying those words, for which I shall bless you while I live."

Again their hands met—this time in earnest kindness; for, on both sides, there was gratitude; and if they parted with heavy hearts, surely the burden of either was lighter than when they met.

The funeral procession reached Minstercombe late one night; and early the next morning the burial-rites were read, by her own husband, over

Ida Luttrell. None of the tenantry received any intimation of the ceremony, and only a few old servants of the family, besides Chetwynde, were present. The latter had tried to dissuade his friend from performing the last duties himself; but Geoffrey was firm. He went through the service with wonderful composure; but Paul remarked that he read it throughout in one even monotone, quite unlike his usual voice, as if he were afraid of lingering, or hesitating over particular passages.

When all was over, and the two friends were left alone in the church, they both stood silent, for awhile, gazing earnestly on the broad marble slab that had just fallen into its place again above the last of the dead Luttrells. At last, Geoffrey spoke, in a voice hushed and low, as befitted the place and time.

"Paul—I am not mad, now. I believe I do justice to every one—to Maurice Dering above all. In what has passed, I *can* see, now, the hand of God—not of any man. But I want you to promise one thing, here, for him as well as for yourself. I have asked it of Philip already

—it is, that neither you nor he will ever speak of *her* to each other, or to me."

Paul gave the promise as simply as it was asked: then he moved quietly away, leaving Luttrell quite alone. Geoffrey followed soon after; but he shut himself up in his own room, and Chetwynde saw him no more that day. Indeed, the latter guessed that utter solitude was what his friend most desired just then: so the next evening, without attempting pretexts or excuses, he departed. If he had feared of the other's misunderstanding him, the long cordial pressure of Luttrell's hand would have reassured him. They parted, perhaps faster friends than ever.

The manner of the interment caused no small talk in the country-side: to say nothing of the haste, which many considered indecorous, it was thought strange that the widower should himself have performed the burial-rites: vague rumours were floating about for some time afterwards, and, had it not been for Geoffrey's personal popularity, it might have gone hard with the fair fame of the dead. But all liked the parson of Minstercombe, even if they revered him not; so the rustic marvel-mongers had mercy on him in his bereavement, and forbore from tampering with his young wife's memory. Even that ancient dame, whose dignity poor Ida once so mortally offended, betrayed no exultation at seeing her prophecies of evil so speedily fulfilled.

It may seem to many absurdly unnatural that a woman holding Ida Luttrell's position in the social scale, should have indulged in such deliberate malice, with so much certain risk, so little probable gain. She must have known how infinitely faint was her chance of ever tempting Maurice to sin; and—were it otherwise—how unlikely it was that Georgie would in anywise interfere with her designs. But the self-deception of some of those wilful, passionate natures, even when joined to a keen, cool intellect, is one of the most marvellous of moral phenomena. Ida was possessed with the fixed idea, that her cousin had once stood betwixt herself and her heart's desire, and might do so again; so, exaggerating the chances of the past, no less than those of the future—she resolved to remove her rival from her path once and for ever.

Of a truth, destructiveness, without any apparent object, *is* somewhat hard to realise or comprehend. Yet, I have heard of an eminently respectable matron, against whom scandal never dared to whisper, who—finding by chance a poisoned shaft in her quiver—forbore not to send it straight to its mark, though the enemy whom she wished to dishonour could never harm any creature more; and, indeed, was even then waiting for death, that came within the week.

CHAPTER XIII.

DARKEST OF ALL.

HAS any one of us forgotten the evil Spring, when there swept over this country of ours a blast from the East—fatal to many households as the wind from the wilderness that smote the banqueting-hall in Uz—chilling to many hearts as the deadly Sarsar? Have we forgotten how, with each successive mail, the wrath and the horror grew wilder; till the sluggish Anglo-Saxon nature became, as it were, possessed by a devil, and through the length and breadth of the land—from Shetland to Scilly, from Cape Clear to the Nore—there went up one awful cry for vengeance? I speak of the Spring, when the news of the Great Mutiny came home.

Chetwynde chanced to be at his club on the evening of the day when the first definite or credible tidings arrived. He and others were talking over what they had just heard,—still hardly realizing the possibility of such things being true—when there came in a friend of Paul's, a high Government official, who, of all men, was likely to be possessed of the last and most accurate information.

Harry Thurlowe's jovial round face was graver and gloomier than any one there had ever seen it: he shook his head ominously, while he 'hoped that the reports were much exaggerated;' but seemed very loth to enter upon the subject, and evaded inquiries with more than diplomatic reserve. When he extricated himself at last from the anxious group, he took Chetwynde's arm, and drew him away; never speaking till they were in one of the card-rooms, which at that hour was quite deserted. Then said Thurlowe, clearing his throat, huskily——

"By G—d, Paul, it's all true; and there's worse to come yet, I fear. What we do know is bad enough. This is why I wanted to speak to you, especially. You would do much for Maurice Dering, wouldn't you?"

"I would do *anything*, only too readily,"

Chetwynde answered: his tone was measured and calm as usual, but a sick, cold apprehension began to rise within him.

"Then you must break to him the heaviest news—if I have guessed rightly—that man can bring to man," the other said. "I heard all about his adventure with the bear, and how he was nursed at Drummond's hunting-bungalow. I heard, too, a vague rumour of his being engaged to Alice Leslie. It's more than likely. I saw a good deal of her while she was in England —she was always with my nieces—I can't fancy anything more loveable. Well, one of the places from which we have *certain* news, is—Darrah. The mutineers made about their earliest onslaught there: the next morning not an European was left alive in the cantonment: what devilries were done before the massacre was complete, the Fiend only knows."

There was a terrible pause for several seconds; then Chetwynde—whose face was whiter than it had been when he waited for Annesleigh's fire— hissed through his clenched teeth—

"You ask me to tell Maurice Dering *this?*"

"I do," the other answered firmly. "Because, in a case like this, if one single pang can be lightened, or one ounce taken off from the weight of the first shock, a man's best friend ought not to shrink from his duty. You *can* do it, too; I don't think I could. I'm not braver than my neighbours; yet, I believe, I'd sooner face a battery."

Paul Chetwynde gathered himself together, with one of those physical efforts that only faintly typify the exertion of will going on within.

"You are thoroughly right, Thurlowe. I'd do it, if it killed me. But we never know how weak we are till our manhood is really tried. The time is fearfully short. Maurice comes to town to-night. I'll go straight to his rooms, and wait for him. I won't give my cowardice a chance. Once there, I must speak."

And Chetwynde did straightway as he said.

Few men in their lifetime are destined to pass such a miserable hour, as that which elapsed before Dering's return. Paul was temperate, as a rule, beyond his fellows; he drank more brandy during those sixty minutes than he had ever done in the same number of hours. He drank, not to give unnatural strength to his nerve, but simply to drive back the feeling of bodily weakness that seemed to chill and sicken him. His heart throbbed, like a frightened girl's, as Maurice's quick, firm step sounded on the stairs.

One glance at Chetwynde's face was enough for Dering. You remember he was quick at guessing its expression.

"In God's name, what has happened?" he said.

Paul came forward and laid his two hands on the other's shoulders, as if he himself stood in need of support: then—without a syllable of preparation—in a dull mechanical voice, like that of one answering a mesmerist's questions, he repeated Thurlowe's news, almost word for word; only, not hinting at the possibility of other outrage than death. Now this was as different from the fashion in which he had intended to discharge his wretched embassage as it is possible to conceive. In no way could the news have been broken more abruptly; yet, perhaps, it was best so. 'If our hope and happiness are to perish,' say most of us, 'let them die without long preamble before, or elaborate consolation after the blow.' True and natural were the words of the bereaved bride in that pitiful romance of 'Sir Peter Harpedon's Ending,' when the page faltered in his sorrowful message:—

> I pray you tell your tale;
> And go on speaking fast, and heed me not
> Whether I scream or fall.

Many years ago, when in Tyrolese forests it was war to the knife between the keepers and marauders of the game—when men, on either side, were slaughtered without a word of warning—one of the former, going his rounds, saw the torso of a notorious poacher rise slowly up, on the opposite side of a broad ravine, till the whole figure stood upright against the sky-line. The forester hesitated awhile, simply because the distance was very long; then he drew a steady bead on the centre of his enemy's chest. The poacher never sprang at the shot; but opened his vest slowly, and gazed, for a full minute, into his own bosom, with a vacant wonder; then he fell down stone-dead.

After that same fashion did Maurice Dering bear himself, when those tidings struck him to the heart. He withdrew his shoulder—not abruptly—from the pressure of Chetwynde's hand, and, retreating backward a pace or two, sate quietly down, gazing into the other's face with a surprise too stupified for horror. That gaze lasted longer than Paul could bear it; for the first time in his life, he felt his nerve utterly failing him. He laid his hand again on Dering's shoulder, and shook it almost roughly.

"Maurice—Maurice—don't stare so horribly; and—say something; or I shall think we are both going mad."

The other passed his tongue twice or thrice over his lips, that seemed to have grown suddenly parched and black.

"Did—did they kill the women—*first?*"— he said, in a hoarse whisper.

Paul shivered, as he answered—

"I trust in God, it was so; but, no one knows."

(And no one ever did know. They heard in after days how hard old Patrick Drummond had died; like one of his own wild-boars, fighting and goring to the last: but round the agony of sweet Alice Leslie and her mother—perhaps in mercy—was drawn a cloud of uncertainty, never lifted in this world.)

"Because," Maurice went on, still in the same unnatural whisper, "that dying woman, in her curse, spoke of dishonour as well as death. She's satisfied now, or she's hard to please." He broke into a sort of ghastly laugh, worse to hear than any groan.

"For God's sake don't think of such things at this moment," the other interrupted. "I cannot comfort you, or even tell you not to despair; but keep your senses if you can: there's work—and bitter hard work—before you yet."

Dering's eyes were fixed no longer in that vacant glazed stare; yet he hardly seemed to catch the meaning of Chetwynde's words, and began muttering to himself like one in a reverie.

"Her dream—yes, now I understand her dream: the pit, and the devils below, and the devil above who thrust her down. No wonder she was frightened: and I left her to her fate —such a fate—to come back and flatter that old man for his money. Ah, my darling! my darling!—if I had only been there to save you, or slay you with my own hand, and follow you quickly. We should have felt no pain— then. And now—what does it matter if my brain should turn? Is there anything left to live for?"

"Nothing left to live for?" a deep voice said in his ear. "Then you do not care for vengeance? If I had your sword-arm to strike with, I would have a life for every hair in that sweet innocent's head; though, I swear, I believe she died stainless. The God that she worshipped would never have looked on such horrors as you fear, and held His hand. I don't speak canonically, because I speak as I feel; but even Geoffrey would hardly preach forgiveness of injuries here."

Now if Chetwynde had been thrice as good a Christian as he was ever likely to be, it is probable he would have spoken in much the same strain, though more guardedly. His first object was to rouse Maurice from his stupor, at any cost; and he knew that certain diseases, of mind and body, can only be touched by small doses of dangerous poisons. The dose worked, now at all events, effectually. When Dering rose to his feet, that vague, vacant look had left his face; it was possessed by an expression—that became its habitual one in the after-time,—an expression, neither savage nor moody, nor even melancholy, but darkly determined, as of a man who, through all the changes and chances of life, keeps a single purpose before him, unswervingly.

"You are right," he said; "we shall have time enough to make our moan when our work is done. Forgiveness of injuries? Why, if all the angels of Heaven—save *one*—stood in my way and warned, I would walk on straight to my revenge. Look here, Paul,—I'm not a natural philosopher, and I can't explain these things. I only know that I'm as much changed within the last few minutes as if I had been born over again. I've always tried to do my best, for others not less than myself; I never hurt a living creature wilfully, till I shot that poor devil, who liked me after all. *You* know how that came off. Perhaps I deserved to be punished for it; but—not like this. I'll go my own way, now, and fight for my own hand. Do you think I am raving, still? Feel my pulse, it's as steady as your own, I dare swear."

As steady? Ay, steadier far than was Chetwynde's that night, or many a night after; for, indeed, all these repeated calamities, falling upon those very dear to him, told heavily upon Paul's organization. The very fact of his being bound to look on as a passive spectator, was inexpressibly trying. Instead of the cold composure that had been its habitual expression, people began to remark a restless dissatisfaction and anxiety on his face: there were many comments thereon, and his friends or acquaintances shook their heads ominously, hinting that 'Chetwynde had certainly been speculating, and had got into difficulties.' So, in truth, he had; but the speculations and the difficulties were not such as the world ever gave him credit for.

Paul himself never could remember, what were the last words that passed that night between himself and Dering. He had a vague recollection of their having spoken with tolerable calmness of Maurice's immediate departure. But, as he walked homewards, a certain relief mingled with intense depression : it was very much the feeling of a man who has lost a ruinous stake, and paid it on the spot. For, as has been aforesaid, Paul's cynicism would not stand wear and tear; it was apt to break down just at those critical seasons when it would have been useful, if not creditable, to its possessor.

Dering did not lose an hour in making the necessary arrangements for departure. These were easily concluded; for the War Office is not unaccommodating when a man wishes to rejoin his regiment, in the most peaceful times. Except when forced to go out on business, he never left his rooms till after nightfall, when he would walk for an hour or so with Chetwynde. Even to Paul he would not speak again about the past: their talk was all of the immediate future: no other of Maurice's friends saw him face to face.

That was a time rife with terrible reports and rumours; some of them utterly groundless, all more or less vague. Somehow or another it began to be whispered about—though no one could give his authority—that Dering was among the chief of those who had awful wrongs to avenge. Amidst all the bustle of their own preparations, when the starting of the reinforcements was a question of hours, some of his old comrades found time to compassionate Maurice, and to speculate as to how he would bear himself in the coming struggle.

"You mark me, now," one man said, who knew him well. "We're none of us going out in an amiable frame of mind; but, when Maurice gets well among 'em, I'll back him to do more damage than any other three. Pluck has got nothing to do with it. I've watched his eye often enough; if there's not a wicked devil under all that *bonhommie* of his, I'm very much mistaken. It's not for nothing, he's shut himself up, ever since the news came in. Before many months are over, you'll see if in Pandy-killing he don't beat all he has done among the big game."

And this—more elegantly expressed—was also the opinion of the chiefest club-oracles at The Bellona.

Three days before he started, Maurice Dering went down to Marston Lisle. Though he had been there on one fatal evening, you will remember that he had not seen the Gascoignes since the night before the duel. This time he only stayed a few hours; but they were very painful ones. All pretext for reticence was, unhappily, over now; so Philip told his wife of the terrible woe that had stricken Dering, as soon as he himself heard of it. It would be difficult to say, which of the two was the most grieved and horrified. Yet, like Chetwynde, they were wise enough to abstain from set forms of consolation. Indeed, had either been so tempted, the first glance into Maurice's face would have checked the meditated condolence. It wore the same dark, determined look of which I have already spoken; the lips, once so mobile in mirth, rarely now unbraced themselves; the eyes that used to flash and glitter so readily, were fixed in a strange earnestness, as if they were gazing intently on some object in the far distance.

The farewells were very trying. Both Philip and Georgie were aware that Maurice was going into the front of the battle, where he would be the last to spare himself. Dering did not seem to reckon on the possibility of his life being cut short before he had finished what was appointed for him to do; but he did not dissemble from his friends, that it would probably be long before they saw his face again.

During the few minutes that he spent alone with Gascoigne, Maurice made no allusion to his loss; neither had Philip courage to do so. Had it been a bereavement, such as is common to man, it is probable that neither would have so avoided the subject; about this one there was a black, indefinite horror which set it beyond the pale of ordinary human sorrows. They spoke rather of their old friendship, which—though not by free-will of either—seemed to both very near an ending. For the health of the one was so precarious—though no change for the worse had been perceptible of late—the risks that the other was about to incur so heavy, that the chances against their meeting again in this life were more than even.

"It ought to have brought us better luck," Philip said at last, pensively. "I don't suppose four men have often lived so much and so long together, as you and I and Paul and Geoffrey, without a sullen look or sharp word passing among them. We did have some pleasant times, too, before these dark days came upon us. Is it not strange that, a year ago, three of us could not have seen one little white cloud in the sky; and now, over us all, it is bitter-black and stormy? Yes, over all; for, I believe Paul's skeleton is as ghastly as any of ours, and of far more ancient date. He never told you of it? No: I thought not: he never would have told me, if he had not wished to make me use his help unscrupulously whenever I needed it. I said then, that he was more to be pitied than myself: I say now, that my burden is the lightest of all."

"All are heavy enough, it seems to me," the other answered, "only you carry yours more easily. Yes—our boat was fairly manned, as you say, and we pulled well together; but I'm fatalist enough, *now*, to be certain that she never could have escaped wreck. I wonder who was the Jonah? Myself, I do believe; for of late there's a curse or a blight on all my good intentions; they crop up as different as possible from the seed I meant to sow. Whenever I try to keep anyone out of a pit, I only fall headlong in myself. I'm nearly weary of it all."

It was Maurice Dering who was speaking; outwardly—the same Maurice who, a few months ago, came back from the East, with so much cordial cheeriness about him, that, in his presence, neither Philip nor Philip's familiars could despond. The change was almost as terrible as that of which the old Norse legend tells, when the corpse of slain Asmundur rose up possessed by a fiend.

Philip Gascoigne's thin white fingers closed round the other's wrist, in remonstrance and pleading.

"Ah, Maurice, our last words must needs be dreary; but don't let them be desperate or unjust. For you *are* unjust, not to yourself only, but to me and mine. Have you forgotten what we owe you? Don't you know that my little Cecil has been taught to pray for you, ever since he could say 'Our Father' plainly? Would he ever have been born, but for you? Surely that life saved, may stand against the life taken in your rashness. I don't attempt to excuse you about poor Annesleigh; simply because I can't at all comprehend it. I think you must have been out of your senses at the time; and I know you have since repented bitterly."

Philip spoke in utter simplicity without the faintest glimmering of the truth, and without an idea of entrapping Dering into an avowal. Very differently would he have spoken, had he guessed that the debt, since he set it down, had been more than doubled—that Maurice had risked less to save Georgie's life, than he risked to save her honour.

Many men would have been tempted to confess all, if it were only to leave no false impressions on an old friend's mind when they were parting, most likely for ever. But Maurice felt no such impulse; he held it better to leave everything as it then stood: it seemed to him that, here in England, he had no further concern with the affairs of friend or foe. Only there was a quaint, conscious look on his face as he answered, that did not quite escape Philip.

"Don't let us talk about debts, or gratitude, or I shall begin to think that I have never been half thankful enough for the hundreds of pleasant hours that I have spent at Marston. The truth is, that between *us*, thanks are absurd formalities. If anything could make me feel less dreary, it would be the certainty that never a word has passed between us that had better have been left unsaid; and that neither you nor I have once had a thought of the other, that we need repent of, now. There—I hear your wife's step: she is to go with me while I say 'good bye' to

The Moor. Then I shall just have time, to say it to you all; and—you must let me go."

A thick fall of black lace shaded all the upper part of Mrs. Gascoigne's face, but the traces of weeping were very plain to discern; and as she walked to the stables by Dering's side, the heavy drops still kept brimming over. Neither spoke till they came to the loose-box where The Moor was standing. Maurice had hunted him all through the winter, and the horse had gone in his usual brilliant form; but directly the season was over, he returned to his quarters at Marston; and there he stood, just the same picture of a weight-carrier as ever—not a hair the worse for four months' hard work, and not looking a day older than when he beat Lady Agatha for the Gold Cup at Walmington. Georgie had only spoken the truth when she wrote—"He likes me much the best, now;" for though the good horse came to Maurice when he was called, his broad, bright eye turned first to the fairer face, and his nostrils sought the caress of the softer hand.

Maurice smiled, more sadly than bitterly.

"So you really have changed service, old man?" he said. "That's just as it should be; for I was going to transfer it. Georgie" (he had addressed her thus more than once since his return, but always in Philip's presence), "it's rather late in the day to ask you to take The Moor for your own. But you won't mind that. He's as steady as a church, and I hope will carry you pleasantly and safely for many, many years; though he looks too much for you. Will you have him?"

Even in that dreary moment, the horse-language came naturally to Dering's lips; but it did not sound absurd or inconsistent to his hearer. Georgie never was farther from mirth than when she murmured her half-intelligible thanks.

Dering had passed his arm round the big brown neck that was curved over his shoulder, and was leaning his cheek against it, apparently musing. Indeed, a train of thought, strangely connected, though infinitely rapid, possessed him then.

He saw Georgie, as he saw her for the very

first time, when, as she swept down The Row at a slinging canter, his eyes, among many others, followed, admiringly, the lithe, graceful figure, and the bright hair glinting back the sun-rays like burnished metal. He saw her as she had ridden by his side—slowly, so slowly—through the green lanes leading to the gate-tower of Harlestone, when the net of her witcheries so nearly trapped him; he saw her, white and distraught with terror, as she was when The Moor's last effort brought him alongside, not a second too soon: he saw her, as she had looked up at him through her tears, just after he had clasped the marriage-gift upon her arm, when all real peril was over, and a fast friendship was signed and sealed.

He thought of her in all these phases, without the quickening of a pulse or the thrilling of a nerve, just as a man in the extremity of old age may look upon the loves and wars of his hot youth. Nevertheless, the lines of Dering's face did surely soften; though Georgie could only catch a partial glimpse of it, she guessed intuitively at the change in his mood. It emboldened her to draw nearer, and lay a little trembling hand on his shoulder.

"If you would only let me pity you!" she whispered. "I would have loved her so dearly!"

Then one of those strange revulsions of feeling, that puzzle acutest physiologists, came over Dering. Though there never had been a shadow of rivalry between those two, perhaps, at any other time, Georgie Gascoigne was the last person alive that Maurice would have allowed to allude to Alice Leslie. But now, those sweet, plaintive tones went straight to his heart—soothing while they saddened inexpressibly: it seemed as if no lips were worthier than *hers*, to make moan over his dead darling. One sob after another shook his stalwart frame from neck to heel; and, as he turned his head yet more aside, Georgie saw the big drops stealing through his locked fingers. She felt almost frightened at what she had done—indeed, the tears of manhood, seen for the first time, are to womanhood very terrible—and drew back into the outer stable. There she sat down on a low bench, and herself gave way to the weeping that she had hitherto partially controlled.

In a little while, a hand was laid softly on her shoulder: she looked up into a face once more hard and stern. I would I could say, that that brief yielding to natural emotion had wrought in Dering's heart for lasting good. It was not so: neither to man nor woman was it given, ever again to see his eyes grow moist, in tenderness, or compassion, or sorrow. Ah me! As with the winter without, so it is with the winter within: the second frost always lasts the longest.

Maurice spoke quite calmly.

"I am not in the least ashamed that you have seen my weakness—if it be a weakness. Only I cannot speak of *her*, even to you, who are so good and kind. But I am not the less grateful: you will remember that, whenever you think of me? We shall none of us quite forget, I know. If I never come back, you'll show Cecil over our racing-ground in The Chase sometimes, and tell him I'd have taught him to ride, if everything had not gone wrong. I think Philip is getting stronger; and I do believe there are bright days in store for all three of you—to say nothing of dear Aunt Nellie. I would say—'God grant it.' But—I dare not: my good wishes of late have been fearfully like witches' prayers. Now, let us go back: I fear I have overstayed my time."

The last farewells were very brief, as all such should be. Yet, though there was little demonstrative grief, and no wailing aloud, few sadder groups could have been found than the one gathered that afternoon on the steps of Marston Lisle. Only one circumstance deserves to be recorded.

Dering had said very affectionate adieus to Aunt Nellie, who was quite as fond of him as if he had been her blood-relation; and came to where Mrs. Gascoigne stood with her boy by her side. Maurice clasped both her hands, warmly: while he held them, she looked up at him, with the soft bright eyes, that had not meant coquettish mischief for many a day, and said—" Kiss me—once, before you go."

He stooped, and his lips just brushed the smooth white forehead: never, I think, was caress asked for or bestowed in purer simplicity, since gorse began to bloom.

The heir of Marston Lisle, though a very important personage in his own family circle, has scarcely been alluded to in these pages. He had inherited the beauty of both his parents in about equal shares; it was no wonder they were so proud of him. Cecil was not at all afraid of swine, or kine, or turkeys, or sudden noises, or other terrors to which infancy is liable; but he was decidedly shy, and slow in overcoming his dread of strangers. Of his special favourites he was curiously fond. Chief amongst these stood Maurice Dering. The child had seen comparatively little of him; but had taken to him from the very first, and would sit on his knee for hours, listening to stories about bears and tigers—the more delightful because scarcely half comprehended: he would be quite contented, too, when his friend was talking to others; finding, apparently, sufficient amusement in winding his tiny soft hands in and out of the profuse chestnut beard against which his own curls were resting.

Cecil had watched the leave-taking with a

sorrowful wonder in his great dark eyes: he could understand every one being sorry at the departure of his favourite; but why every one was more sorry *this* time, he could not understand. The caress bestowed upon his mother puzzled him most of all. *That* was clearly out of the ordinary run of adieus, and contrary to all precedents: possibly, across his infantine mind, there shot some vague idea of indecorum. At any rate he deemed it time to come to the front, and claim his share of the good things that were going: he pulled his mother's dress, and signified, in his baby-language, rather an imperious desire to be embraced immediately.

Maurice caught up the child in his strong arms, and gazed for a second or two earnestly into the face, almost too refined already in its delicate beauty; then he drew Cecil slowly towards him. But, as the latter stretched out his slender arms to clasp his friend's neck, the others saw Dering shiver all over as if a sudden chill had struck him: he thrust the child back, before the little rosebud-mouth touched his own; and set him down almost abruptly, muttering—

"No—not as I am. It would be cruel—he would never thrive."

As if he could not trust himself farther, Maurice wrung Gascoigne's hand once—hard—as he passed him, and, springing into the cart that was waiting, drove hastily away.

Poor Cecil stood for a minute transfixed with wonder and grief: then he broke out into lamentation loud and long. So Maurice Dering departed from Marston Lisle with the sound of wailing in his ears, though that wailing was but a child's; ay, and the first sweep of the road brought him full in sight of that shrubbery, where a few months agone the fair white corpse pressed down the autumn leaves.

Does any one *quite* disbelieve in omens?

In after days,—as they heard with a shudder of the terrible deeds of semi-judicial vengeance that made Dering's name a by-word even in that bloody time,—Cecil's parents guessed why he had forborne to set his lips on their child's innocent brow, and did the unhappy man justice in their hearts.

CHAPTER XIV.

NO QUARTER.

ALL that winter through, Geoffrey Luttrell had shut himself up at Minstercombe. Though no direct explanation had passed between them, Dering knew that his friend held him entirely blameless in the matter of Ida, and several letters had been exchanged in the old spirit of kindliness. So he was not surprised, on his return from Marston, at finding a note to say that Geoffrey was in town, and would call early on the following morning: indeed, Maurice would have been bitterly disappointed if he had gone away without one last sight of that honest face.

There was no shadow of distrust or reproach between them, now; nevertheless, the meeting of those men was somewhat strange. Death brought them together, as death had parted them;

only, this time, the fair corpse lay—not at their feet, but a thousand leagues away.

As Geoffrey held Maurice's hand, and gazed wistfully into his eyes, he felt his own grief grow faint and dim in presence of a more awful sorrow: his voice shook and faltered as he said, below his breath——

"I guessed it had gone hard with you, but—not so hard as this."

Any outward evidence of misery he was prepared to meet; it was the set dark look of the worn face that shocked Luttrell so painfully: he thought the wildness of agony would have been better than that. He felt it would be almost a mockery, to talk of resignation or submission here. Yet he was brave in his vocation, as in all things else: he did try to speak, as his conscience commanded; though the sentences were not very coherent or clear.

Dering did not interrupt, but listened absently and indifferently; as a man will do whose mind is thoroughly made up, and does not think it worth while to discuss the question: it was evident that the words affected him very much as if they had been uttered from the pulpit. The poor parson's heart sank within him, as he felt that his simple theology was nearly exhausted, without one foot of ground gained.

"You are right, I am sure," Dering said at last. "Only you might as well be talking in an unknown tongue, as far as my comprehending you goes. I suppose it is a question of intellect; and mine is very dull of late."

"It is *not* a question of intellect," the other retorted, eagerly. "It is a question of faith. Cannot you see that our only safeguard, in this world, against despairing infidelity is, to accept *all* Divine decrees without questioning or sifting them? If we cannot bring ourselves to believe —bitterly hard as it may be—that all blows dealt by His hand are dealt in mercy, we are not far from the state of the lost."

Dering rose up upon his feet, and confronted the other, with an evil light in his eyes.

"Look here," he said, hoarsely. "If you want me to listen to you, you had better drop that word 'mercy.' You may go too far in your special pleading, though your case be ever so good and strong. I'm not an infidel, and I don't want to become a blasphemer; nor do I dispute the Creator's right to work His will with His own creatures. You may say the Great Plague was sent in 'mercy' if you choose, and I won't contradict you; but I will—if you say it was in 'mercy' that my innocent darling was given up to those unchained devils."

He gnashed his teeth as he spoke, and his moustache grew white and wet with foam. Geoffrey frowned, though there was no anger on his sad face.

"I cannot hear such words without rebuking them. I must seem to speak hardly and harshly, when, God knows, I mean far otherwise. Have you not heard that there are such things as chastisements and expiations on this side of the grave? Can you say, that you have incurred none of these?"

Maurice bent his head, half assentingly, half humbly.

"I have thought of that," he answered —"thought of it many times, since I held up Annesleigh's head, while he was dying. But I reckoned that the punishment of the blood-shedder would have fallen upon me. What harm had *she* done?"

That other voice came in—deep and slow and solemn, as a funeral-bell tolling.

"Only to the man after His own heart did God give the choice of atonement. What harm had those little children done, who were stoned to death in the Valley of Achan?"

Though the dark hour was heavy on Maurice Dering, those words impressed him with awe, real, albeit momentary.

He felt that it was the Truth he heard, however hard to understand; though fresh pangs shot through his rankling wound, he knew that the priest was bound to use cautery, where the friend would fain have poured in balm.

"Have it your own way," he said, rather wearily; "at least for the present. What is it you would have me do?"

Quick and stern was Luttrell's answer.

"I would have you bear yourself like a Christian man, who had lost all he held dearest; not like a wild beast that has lost its young.

Strike, as starkly as you please, in the front of the battle; I don't ask you to give quarter there; for I am of the same flesh and blood as you. But I do ask you, not to make duty a mere cloak for private revenge; I ask you not to slay the innocent with the guilty; not to turn slaughter into massacre. Do I ask too much? The lesson you have had already might teach you not to forget, again, the old text, 'Vengeance is mine!'"

Dering, still standing, laid his clenched hand upon the table before him, with no apparent violence; yet you might have seen the veins and sinews starting out, one by one.

The honest parson's heart sank within him; he read the deadly meaning of the desperate face aright, and knew that warning and pleading, now, would be equally vain.

"I quite understand you," Maurice said, in a slow, suppressed voice. "You think I ought to temper justice with mercy, and show discrimination in punishment, and be generous in victory, and—all the rest of it. My dear good Geoffrey! Don't you see you are speaking, after your own light, to a blinded man? Once more, I do not deny the Almighty's right to deal with his creatures after his pleasure—to save or to destroy. He may make me powerless at any instant to harm a worm. I know that. But I know something else, too. If one mutineer, who could have been within a hundred miles of Darrah, on that accursed day, when once fairly within my arm's length or in my power, takes his life away with him, why—your theology is all astray; for the age of miracles is not past."

Luttrell rose in his turn; feeling more miserably despondent than he had done since the night of Ida's funeral.

"Don't say another word. You have said enough already to make me wish I had written 'Farewell' instead of speaking it. Poor Maurice—for I do pity you with my whole heart—what you have suffered is bad enough, but what you will suffer is worse still. Where will you find help, like that which you are wilfully casting away? I can do no more. As you are now, I dare not even ask God to bless you; but I *can* ask Him to turn and save you, and to forgive you, too.

You will never be forgotten, while I have strength to pray. You will be sorry, some day, when you remember how your last words grieved me; for I never vexed you knowingly in my life; and never spoke sharply—but once, when my senses were gone. Yet I think, we surely shall meet again: it seems to me that both you and I have much work to do before we die."

The two strong hands were knit together for a full minute, in an honest grip, that was worth a dozen protestations or promises: and truer friends never parted on earth, though just now the horror of darkness brooded over one—if not both—of their souls.

It was from Luttrell that Chetwynde first heard of this interview, for Maurice scarcely alluded to it, beyond remarking, that 'it was very good of Geoff. to come all that way to say good-bye.' The parson did not go much into details; and he was the less disposed to do so, when he saw that Paul's sympathies were enlisted already—not on his side.

In that same week Maurice paid a parting visit to his god-father above-mentioned, in obedience to a very pressing summons. The old man was arbitrary and capricious both by nature and habit, but neither hard nor cold-hearted: he was dreadfully shocked at hearing of the fearful termination of all the matrimonial schemes that he discussed with his *protégé;* and glanced up at his god-son when the latter came in, nervously—almost timidly; as if he feared, that he might in some way be held accountable for what had happened.

But, changed as Maurice was, he had not yet become unjust or ungrateful; he remembered that Mr. Grimstone had acted considerately enough throughout, and had not exacted more deference than he could fairly claim: so the first greetings, though melancholy of course, were not less kindly than usual.

After awhile the old man began to press Maurice to defer, if only for a little, his return to India; pleading, as before, his own failing health, and growing incapacity to look after his affairs.

"Look here, Maurice,"—he said, at last— "here's my will: I shall never alter it now. If you read it, you'll see you really ought to stay and help me: I shan't trouble you many months—or weeks—longer. You are only taking care of your own: you are my sole heir."

The words were probably meant rather in rough consolation, than as a bribe; for, though hardly a miser, Mr. Grimstone had all his life long been wont to consider golden salve an infallible remedy for all ills of body or mind. But the kindness, if so it were intended, was clumsily offered—unhappily timed. Maurice frowned darkly.

"I sail on Tuesday next," he said. "If it were to settle the fortunes of England instead of yours, I would not stay another hour. As for your health—I sincerely hope it is better than you fancy, and that you will enjoy your riches for years to come yet. I pray you do not think of me in disposing of them. I have enough already to last me for my life; and, somehow, I feel as if I could no more touch your money than if there were blood on it. Yes—I know: it wasn't your fault, any more than it was poor

Patrick Drummond's. But if *he* had not told me it was my duty to come home and consult *you*, I should have been thousands of miles nearer to my darling's murderers, now, if I had not been near enough to die with her. Please don't say another word; my temper's not what it used to be; but I've not forgotten yet, that you were always kind to my father and to me. Let us part in peace."

The dark resolute expression of Maurice's face, and his harsh, stern tones, fairly disconcerted, if they did not alarm, Mr. Grimstone, in whose austere presence very few had permitted themselves to indulge in violence, or even emotion. He was rather relieved when, after a few more words of ordinary leave-taking, the door closed behind his god-son: yet he looked after him wistfully.

"Poor boy, poor boy!" he muttered. "I'm afraid his brain is rather turned. I don't wonder—though I never was in love myself—if she was like her picture. I wish he had left it with me: I daren't ask him for it now. Well —well; I suppose I shall have to die alone.

It's hard: but I shan't alter my will, for all that."

Nor did he.

Chetwynde accompanied Dering to Southampton, and saw him on board. They had little opportunity for confidential talk on the journey down, for three of Maurice's comrades were in the same carriage; neither, perhaps, did they desire it. Paul, as you know, was always taciturn, and Maurice, of late, rarely spoke unnecessarily. The deck of a Peninsular and Oriental steamer on the point of starting is never a very exhilarating scene. Till I myself witnessed it, I did not believe that so much quiet weeping could be done, in the midst of such a scramble, and bustle, and uproar. On the present occasion the sight was unusually melancholy; for all those who stayed behind knew right well, what dark perils beyond the sea awaited the outward-bound. They would have to meet fiercer enemies, now, than sun-strokes and jungle-fevers.

The 'Tigris' was on the point of getting under way, and the first warning-bell had rung, when Chetwynde and Dering drew a little aside out of the turmoil, to say the last words. You must be nearly weary of all these leave-takings; but this one was briefest of all: nor on either side was there a trace of emotion: that was all past and done.

"I wonder, how many years it will be before you care to see England again?" Chetwynde remarked. "I dare say I shall get tired of it before you dream of coming back. When those troubles are over, if Philip keeps well—he's stronger: don't you think so?—I've a great mind to come out and see you."

"It would be worth your while," Dering answered, just as calmly. "Though, when these troubles are over, India will be a very different place from what it has been. I shall look forward to it, all the same. Remember —we've only a few minutes more. I shall write to no one but you; and that, very seldom. You may be as liberal as you like with your letters, on that understanding. I'm glad you're going to stay at home, to look after Philip. Paul—perhaps I may not have another chance of telling you—I do trust you, so thoroughly!"

A faint red spot rose on Chetwynde's pale cheek; he bit his lip, half angrily.

"Trust me? It's very good of you to say so, thus late in the day. I've got you into one or two bad scrapes, and never helped you out of one that I remember. And I'm always just out of the line of fire, myself. I swear, I've felt at times shamefully Mazzinian. I can't charge myself with deliberate shirking; but it comes to much the same thing, now, as if I had been both selfish and cowardly. It don't bear thinking of, I can tell you; and it won't be better when you're away."

Maurice looked earnestly into the speaker's face; and, for an instant, a flash of the old frank kindliness lighted up his own, and his eyes sparkled once more.

"Hark, now, Paul," he said, "you'll keep your own judgment, of course, as you always do; but take mine, before I go. I don't like you better, that I know of, than either Philip, or poor, good Geoff. But we've been thrown more together, somehow. Besides, I've always felt we could not be weighed in the same scale as those other two: it might go hard with us if we were. Well—as to all that we are liable for, jointly and severally, I say just this. Whether we acted rightly or wrongly, does not seem as clear to me now, as when my conscience used to speak out plainly: but I know, we meant honestly. I know something more: in the same strait, we'd do the same things over again."

The second warning-bell cut short the rest of their adieus. Five minutes later, Chetwynde was straining his eyes to distinguish the familiar features among the crowd of reverted faces that lined the gangway. No wonder that he failed; for they were not there. Maurice Dering was standing quite aloof from his comrades; and, amongst all those who went forth to 'smite and spare not,' his eyes alone, at the very moment of departure, were bent *forward* with an eager, hungry gaze.

CHAPTER XV.

REQUIESCANT.

In India once more.

This time, you look on a broad, sandy plain, seamed with dry water-courses; with patches of cultivation here and there—all neglected, now; for the tillers of the soil have fled far away from the wrath to come, or are busy elsewhere in bloodier work. Everywhere there are traces of battle or slaughter—rather of the last than the first; for there are not many British uniforms among the tawny corpses that lie strewn about, singly or in groups, beginning to blacken already under the pitiless sun. In truth, a desultory fight became a hot pursuit an hour ago; the quick, dropping musketry begins to be concentrated into something like file-firing in line, about half a league ahead; that is where the river runs, beyond which the Mutineers may find safety for to-day. No wonder they strive so madly to reach the farther shore; for every minute comes a broader flash and a rounder ring; and we know that, in spite of rough ground and ditches like small nullahs, the horse-gunners have thundered to the front, and that their grape is even now lashing up the water into crimson foam.

But with the main scene of slaughter we have nought to do. Turn aside to that clump of forest trees, a full mile to the right. In the centre of this is a tank, and one of those huge masses of nondescript masonry—half temple, half tomb—under which the Rajahs of old times loved to lay their bones. All round the clump is a *cordon* of cavalry—it is small and easily surrounded—too close for a single fugitive to slip through; the remainder of the squadron is dismounted, under the trees immediately round the building.

The lower part of it somewhat resembles a crypt above ground: there are the same low, solid arches and narrow apertures that admit more air than light. From within there comes a confused murmur, sometimes swelling into loud discordance, such as may be heard in any crowd agitated by wrath, or fear, or bewilderment.

Ten score or more of Sepoys and Sowars are penned up within that narrow place of refuge; and corpses, scattered far back on the track, show that many fled not fast enough to escape the sabres led on by Maurice Dering.

Not a shot has been exchanged since the last of the fugitives plunged through the low, dark arch of entrance: almost all had cast their firelocks away in the wild terror of their flight; and such as had still weapons and cartridges left, never dreamt of uselessly irritating their dreadful enemy.

For Dering's name was up already amongst the mutineers: not only did they impute to him supernatural activity in pursuit, and a blood-thirstiness exceeding their own; but they also gave him credit for some charm that made him bullet-proof. The Rohillas had just the same superstition about the famous Brigadier, who for years was the terror of their frontier.

So, after a few minutes of vague uproar within,

a soiled white turban-cloth, flecked here and there with dusky red stains, fluttered out of one of the narrow window slits; and then came forth a cry from many parched throats for 'Quarter' and 'Pardon.'

Maurice strode out alone from among his troopers, till he stood within a few paces of the walls of the tomb. He spoke Hindustani well enough to make himself understood; indeed his speech was very brief and simple: he refused to treat on any terms whatever: the rebels might come forth if they chose, ten at a time; or they might wait the storming where they were. As he spoke the last word, a sharp snap was heard within, followed by a slight scuffle and a smothered groan. One desperate fanatic, who chanced to have kept a loaded rifle, could not resist proving, for the last time, the invulnerability of his terrible enemy: the cap missed fire, and the man was instantly cut down by his comrades,—furious at seeing their faint chance of mercy imperilled.

Dering did not appear to notice the incident; but turned on his heel and walked slowly back to where his charger was held. After a few minutes of noisy deliberation, a hoarse voice from within cried, 'That they would come forth, trusting to the Great Sahib's mercy.' And they began to throw their weapons out of the door and windows, till the ground outside was thickly strewn.

A squad of dismounted troopers marched up to the entrance-arch, ranging themselves on either side of it, before the first ten mutineers came out—their faces blanched to lividness—their great eye-balls rolling wildly—their shining teeth gnashing, as if ferocity had not quite given place to fear. The men walked straight up to the spot where Dering was standing; and, bowing themselves in obeisance, waited his orders. Maurice never spoke, but pointed with his finger towards a certain part of the clump where the trees grew thickest. The prisoners moved off in that direction, without questioning: they were scarcely hidden from view of the tomb-door, when a smothered shriek was heard—drowned in a roll of fire-arms—then a dead silence. Those ten men had marched right into the faces of their appointed executioners.

The miserable wretches within the tomb guessed the fate of their comrades at once; the measured rattle of the carbines was significant enough. A tumult of howls and shrieks arose; when it partly subsided, many cried out, 'that no more would come forth, the Sahib might kill them, where they were.'

It is better to stop here.

Do you remember the 'murder grim and great' that avenged beautiful Hypatia? *This* carnage was worse a thousand-fold: for it was wrought, not under the fresh clear night-sky, but in a close, darkened slaughter-house. Every now and then one of the executioners came staggering out into the open air—drunk and faint with the scent of blood. And Dering stood by—with that dark pitiless look on his face whereof we have before spoken—allowing no pause in the work till it was thoroughly performed.

Reader of mine—do you think all this wildly exaggerated? Perchance you fancy that all the incidents of that awful time were set down in official reports, and recorded by special correspondents. I speak only from hearsay; but I believe there lives a man on the full-pay of our army who saw these things done—very much as I have here described them.

Nevertheless you will augur ill for Maurice Dering's future, when you know that you look on him, now, for the very last time.

The last sketch of the picture-gallery, in which you have been pleased to linger so long, shall not be so repellant or gloomy.

It is a warm summer evening; so still, that the leaves of the great beech-trees scarcely rustle in the soft west wind that has been dying away ever since noon. It is an evening made for invalids, no less than for others in stronger health; so, at least, thinks Philip Gascoigne, as he lounges on a pile of cushions, with his fair wife nestling by his side. At the further end of the lawn is Cecil with—it is unnecessary to say—Aunt Nellie in close attendance: he and his favourite playmate have had their last race and gambol for the night; and the child is walking soberly along; his slender arm wound round the huge deer-hound's brindled neck.

But the father and mother are not watching their pet just now. Can you guess why?

Georgie—from one of those sudden impulses that cannot be explained, but are generally safe to follow—has taken heart of grace this night, and made full confession to her husband of the old folly that came so near to guilt.

"Philip, dear"—she went on, when she had told him all, even to that perilous interview in the Géronstère—"I never loved him, as I love you now; nor, I do believe, as I loved you then. Sometimes I think, I did not love him at all. It was a foolish romance with me, at first; and at last I got helplessly frightened. But I was very wicked—so wicked that I don't deserve to be as happy as we are now; for we *are* happy, darling, in our quiet way. Ah,—say you are not angry with me: it was so long ago; and have I not been good since?"

In truth that appeal seemed not altogether needless; for Philip's brow was very grave and thoughtful. But he drew the pretty penitent closer to his side, and kissed her fondly before he answered—

"No, my own darling, I'm not angry; indeed, I have not one reproach ready. Stronger-minded women than my little Georgie have gone down before the fascination that that unhappy man seemed able to exercise—always for evil. To my life's end I shall not cease to thank God for having forbidden the accomplishment of your misery and mine. Yours would have lasted longest, darling: it would have killed me very soon. No; I was not thinking of blaming you. I was thinking, whether Maurice knew of all this when he went out with Annesleigh. Poor fellow! he was so different then from what he must be now—if half the tales are true—that I can't help fearing something of the sort. It's odd, I never suspected it before."

"Oh, I hope—I hope not," Georgie murmured; and her sweet face grew paler than it had been since she began her confession.

Philip could not see his pet distressed, even for a moment, without petting or consoling her.

"Don't fret, darling," he whispered. "It's

only a stupid suspicion of mine, founded on no sort of warranty, that I might just as well have kept to myself. I'll ask Paul about it, the next time I see him."

Gascoigne did question Chetwynde, but got little satisfaction from that saturnine sage, who, as has been aforesaid, was rather prone to indulge in dark sayings and parables.

"Philip," said he, upon this occasion, "you quite surprise me. I always rather envied your memory. Surely, it's not failing you?"

"What on earth do you mean?" the other inquired, rather impatiently.

"Why, I thought 'Lenore' was your favourite ballad; and you seem to have utterly forgotten the *refrain* that I've heard you quote a hundred times—

Lass sie ruh'n, die Todten.

No other word could ever be extracted from Paul on that subject; nor indeed did Gascoigne ever broach it again.

So—as we leave Marston Lisle—if the sky be not radiantly blue above, there is at least promise of fair, calm weather. Pleasant parties gather there not unfrequently; though there are none of the brilliant festivals of the old time. The Duchess of Devorgoil ought to be satisfied; for fair Georgie Gascoigne is discreet—not dignified; that she could never be—as the haughtiest *grande dame* of them all; indeed, certain coquettish matrons, undergoing a *very* gradual process of reformation, point to her as an illustration of what *they* will come to, if they are only let alone.

Philip's health improves rather than otherwise, though he still needs great care; but many indolent people would think it no hardship, to be such an invalid—petted and nursed so tenderly.

It is otherwise at Minstercombe: the curse of childlessness still abides over the heritage of the Luttrells; and will—through this generation—abide. For, though Geoffrey is no longer a recluse, but mixes in quiet society much as he was wont to do, no maiden on her promotion has yet been found audacious enough to aspire to Ida's vacant place. He indulges in field-sports keenly as ever; but, even whilst pursuing these is rather prone to solitude: and the old villagers, who have known him from a boy, shake their heads sometimes, ominously, as they point to the parson's skiff rocking, alone, on the verge of the bay—much too far from land, considering that black cloud-bank to seaward. Some, too, have noticed that there is always a change in his voice when it recites that one petition — 'Forgive us our trespasses, as we forgive them that trespass against us'—and the broad blue eyes turn, with a piteous meaning, towards that corner of the chancel under which the dead Luttrells sleep.

Yet, perchance, even to him there may come peace, at the last.

In Paul Chetwynde there appears little, if any, change: on such as he the battle of life leaves no scars; and they can generally dissemble their wounds, unless stricken to the death. He talks of going to India next year. Maurice Dering's regiment must soon be ordered home; but no one supposes he will accompany it. The pursuit of the big game—the more perilous the better—seems to be his one object, now;

and every hour of leave is spent as far up in the hills as hard riding, to and fro, will carry him. His absences are not much regretted by his regiment: 'he is no use, off parade,' the subalterns say: in truth, that hard, haggard face—not softened by the huge beard, now deeply grizzled, is very fatal to the simple convivialities of his mess-room. His comrades might almost as well have the Egyptian skeleton there.

Of the few subordinate characters in this our drama, it is surely needless to speak : it is more than enough if the principals have carried your interest with them thus far. One word of poor Penrhyn Bligh. Some of his relatives, who had cast him off long ago, took compassion on his desolate destitution, and came to take charge of him; they were just in time to add some comforts to his last brief illness; and they gave him decent burial.

And now, the story of the Quadrilateral is told.

Against fair or open assault, the defenders of that miniature fortress might perchance have held their own. What wonder if the battle went hard against them at the last? If a woman—wily or wicked—be once within the walls, never was ravelin or rampart that long could keep the besiegers at bay.

It was so, before the night that made Rahab the harlot famous among her kind: it will be so, when the Rock is dust that bears Tarpeia's name.

THE END.

BRADBURY AND EVANS, PRINTERS, WHITEFRIARS.

www.ingramcontent.com/pod-product-compliance
Lightning Source LLC
Chambersburg PA
CBHW020800230426
43666CB00007B/789